# 10-Minute Bible Parables for Teens

*Stories of Hope, Growth, and Faith*

## G. JORDAN

© 2025 G. Jordan
All rights reserved.

No part of this publication may be reproduced, stored in a retrieval system, or transmitted in any form or by any means—electronic, mechanical, photocopying, recording, or otherwise—without prior written permission from the publisher.

Scripture quotations are taken from the King James Version (KJV) of the Bible.

This book is a work of devotional encouragement. While the narratives are biblically inspired and based on real people and events from Scripture, the internal thoughts and first-person retellings are creative interpretations meant to highlight spiritual truths.

First Edition: 2025

# Preface

To every teen still figuring life out.
To those questioning their purpose, doubting their worth, or wondering where God fits in the middle of it all.

These stories are for you.
Jesus often taught through parables—simple, everyday stories with deeper meaning hidden inside. Seeds. Sheep. Lost coins. Parties. Builders. Ordinary moments carrying extraordinary truth.
Why? Because God knew we needed reminders. Hope tucked into the ordinary. Lessons hidden in familiar places. And the assurance that, even when life feels complicated, His message is simple:
You are seen.
You are loved.
And your story matters.

This book isn't about perfect answers—it's about discovering God's wisdom in unexpected ways. My prayer is that as you read these parables, they'll challenge you, comfort you, and remind you that faith is a journey of growth, hope, and grace.
You don't have to have it all figured out.
You just have to be willing to listen.

— G. Jordan

# Table of Contents

| | |
|---|---|
| Introduction.................................................................. | 1 |
| How to Use This Book................................................ | 2 |
| 1. I Found My Way Back — The Prodigal Son................. | 3 |
| 2. I Helped My Neighbor — The Good Samaritan.......... | 6 |
| 3. I Buried My Talent — And Regretted It...................... | 9 |
| 4. I Invested What God Gave Me — And Saw It Grow.... | 12 |
| 5. I Showed Mercy — When It Wasn't Expected............ | 15 |
| 6. I Thought I Deserved More — The Workers in the Vineyard....................................................................... | 18 |
| 7. I Built on the Rock — And It Held Firm...................... | 21 |
| 8. I Chose the Wide Road — And Got Lost..................... | 23 |
| 9. I Cared for the Hungry — And Met Jesus There......... | 25 |
| 10. I Let My Light Shine — Even When It Felt Small...... | 27 |
| 11. I Almost Missed the Banquet — But I Said Yes......... | 29 |
| 12. I Refused the Invitation — And Missed Everything... | 31 |
| 13. I Waited for the Bridegroom — And I Was Ready..... | 33 |
| 14. I Ran Out of Oil — And Missed the Door.................. | 35 |
| 15. I Forgave My Debtor — Because I'd Been Forgiven... | 37 |
| 16. I Refused to Forgive — And Paid the Price................ | 39 |
| 17. I Found the Pearl of Great Price — And Let Go of the Rest................................................................................ | 41 |
| 18. I Discovered Treasure in the Field — And Everything Changed........................................................... | 43 |
| 19. I Cast My Net — And God Filled It............................ | 45 |
| 20. I Lost One Sheep — And Searched Until I Found It.. | 47 |
| 21. I Was the Lost Coin — But I Was Never Forgotten.... | 49 |
| 22. I Was a Mustard Seed — Small, But Growing........... | 51 |
| 23. I Was Yeast in the Dough — And God Used Me........ | 53 |
| 24. I Knocked — And the Door Opened.......................... | 55 |
| 25. I Asked — And He Answered.................................... | 57 |
| 26. I Kept Praying — And God Heard Me....................... | 59 |
| 27. I Gave a Cup of Water — And It Mattered................ | 61 |
| 28. I Heard the Wise Builder's Warning — And Changed Course............................................................... | 63 |
| 29. I Hid My Lamp — But the Darkness Grew................ | 65 |
| 30. I Shined My Light — And It Reached Others............ | 67 |
| 31. I Came Empty — But God Filled Me......................... | 69 |
| 32. I Thought I Was Too Late — But God Was Patient... | 71 |
| 33. I Was a Stubborn Soil — But God Kept Planting...... | 73 |
| 34. I Let God's Word Take Root — And It Grew............. | 75 |
| 35. I Ignored the Warning — And Faced the Flood......... | 77 |

| | |
|---|---|
| 36. I Was a Servant Waiting — And the Master Returned.................................................................. | 79 |
| 37. I Fell Asleep on Watch — And Missed My Moment... | 81 |
| 38. I Tried to Hide My Sin — But the Truth Came Out... | 83 |
| 39. I Stayed Humble — And God Lifted Me Up............... | 85 |
| 40. I Took the Best Seat — And Was Sent Away............. | 87 |
| 41. I Sat at the Lowest Place — And Was Invited Higher. | 89 |
| 42. I Judged Others — And Realized I Was Worse.......... | 91 |
| 43. I Removed the Plank — And Saw Clearly.................. | 93 |
| 44. I Tried to Serve Two Masters — And It Broke Me..... | 95 |
| 45. I Chased Riches — And Missed the Kingdom........... | 97 |
| 46. I Trusted God with Little — And He Entrusted Me with More....................................................................... | 99 |
| 47. I Doubted His Return — But He Came Suddenly...... | 101 |
| 48. I Held onto the Seed — And It Never Grew............... | 103 |
| 49. I Let Go — And the Harvest Was Abundant.............. | 105 |
| 50. I Cried for Justice — And God Answered in Time..... | 107 |
| 51. I Knocked and Knocked — And the Judge Heard Me | 109 |
| 52. I Asked for Mercy — And God Gave It Freely............ | 111 |
| 53. I Thought I Was Righteous — But My Pride Was Exposed........................................................................ | 113 |
| 54. I Came Broken — And Walked Away Whole............. | 115 |
| 55. I Wasted My Inheritance — But Found My Father's Arms Open..................................................................... | 117 |
| 56. I Was the Older Brother — And Missed the Celebration.................................................................... | 119 |
| 57. I Looked for the Lost — And Discovered God's Heart | 121 |
| 58. I Believed God's Kingdom Was Near — And I Prepared My Heart.......................................................... | 123 |
| 59. I Planted Seeds — And Watched God Bring the Growth........................................................................... | 125 |
| 60. I Was the Fig Tree — And God Gave Me Another Chance........................................................................... | 127 |
| Closing Note from the Author........................................... | 129 |
| Acknowledgments............................................................ | 130 |
| About the Author.............................................................. | 131 |
| Books in This Series......................................................... | 132 |

# Introduction

Dear Teen Reader,

Life can be complicated. Faith? Even more so. Sometimes, you just wish God would spell it all out—loud, clear, no confusing parts.

But Jesus didn't always teach that way.

Instead, He told stories. Simple, everyday stories. About seeds and sheep. About builders and lost coins. About parties and farmers and people just like us.

At first glance, they sound ordinary. But look closer, and you'll find something deeper—hope, wisdom, and the kind of truth that sticks with you long after the story ends.

That's what this book is about.

Inside these pages, you'll hear familiar parables retold through fresh voices—voices that sound a lot like yours. Struggling, doubting, growing, hoping. Each story is short—about 10 minutes. But the lessons? They last a lifetime.

You'll also find reflection questions, a simple prayer, and a Bible verse after each story to help you pause, process, and connect with God for yourself.

No pressure. No perfect answers. Just space to listen, wonder, and grow.

Because the same God who spoke through parables 2,000 years ago is still speaking today—right into your story.

So slow down. Lean in.
And let His words change you from the inside out.

— G. Jordan

# How to Use This Book

**How to Use This Book**

This isn't a textbook. It's not about memorizing facts or checking off a reading plan. It's about slowing down, listening to the stories Jesus told, and letting them sink into your life.

Here's how to get the most out of it:

▶ **Take your time.**
Each story is short—about 10 minutes—but don't rush. Read one at a time. Let the message settle before you move on.

▶ **Step into the story.**
Every parable is told as if a character is speaking directly to you. Imagine what it felt like to be there. What would you have thought? How would you have responded?

▶ **Pause for reflection.**
After each story, you'll find a few simple questions. You don't need to write your answers down (unless you want to)—just stop and think honestly.

▶ **Pray about it.**
A short prayer is included to help you talk to God. You can pray those words or use them as a starting point for your own.

▶ **Pay attention to the verse.**
Every story ends with a key Bible verse from the King James Version (KJV). These verses help anchor the story's meaning in Scripture.

Most importantly—be real.
Whether your faith feels strong, shaky, or somewhere in between, this book is for you. God speaks through simple stories... and He's speaking to you.

# 1. I Found My Way Back — The Prodigal Son

*(Based on Luke 15:11–24, KJV — The Parable of the Prodigal Son, from the younger son's perspective)*

---

I thought I knew better.

Staying home felt... boring. Following rules? No thanks. I wanted my own life. My own choices. So I did the unthinkable. I asked my father for my share of the inheritance—before he even passed away.

And he gave it to me.

I packed my things and left. No curfews. No chores. No one telling me how to live.

At first, it was everything I dreamed. Parties. Friends. Money that seemed like it would never run out.

But it did.

Soon the friends disappeared. The parties stopped. The only job I could find was feeding pigs—and I was so hungry I wanted to eat their food. That's when reality hit me like a ton of bricks.

I had walked away from everything good. From the people who loved me. From the home that cared for me.

But... maybe... I could go back?

I knew I didn't deserve to be called my father's son. But maybe he'd let me work for him. Be a servant. It was better than starving.

So I walked home, rehearsing my apology the whole way.

But my father... he saw me before I even reached the house.

And he ran.

He wrapped his arms around me. I barely got the words out—my apology, my shame—but he wasn't even listening. He called for new clothes. A ring. A feast.

"My son was lost," he said, "and is found."

I didn't deserve it. But I got it anyway.

Sometimes, we mess up. We run. We think we've gone too far. But the truth is… we can always come home. And when we do, God runs to meet us.

## Reflection Questions:

1. Have you ever made a decision you regretted, like the son in this story?
2. What holds you back from coming back to God after mistakes?
3. How does this story change the way you see God's love?

## Prayer:

Dear God,
Sometimes I feel like I've messed up too much to come back. But You remind me that I'm always welcome in Your arms. Help me not to stay stuck in shame. Give me courage to come home to You—no matter how far I've wandered. Thank You for Your love that never gives up on me.
Amen.

# Key Verse (KJV):

"For this my son was dead, and is alive again; he was lost, and is found."
— *Luke 15:24a*

## 2. I Helped My Neighbor — The Good Samaritan

*(Based on Luke 10:25–37, KJV — The Parable of the Good Samaritan, from the Samaritan's perspective)*

---

I wasn't supposed to care.

See, I'm a Samaritan. And the man lying in the dirt? A Jew. Our people? We don't exactly get along. Years of tension, of walls built between us. But when I saw him on the side of the road—bleeding, barely breathing—I couldn't ignore him.

The others did.

First, a priest walked by. A holy man. You'd think he'd stop. But he crossed to the other side of the road.

Then, a Levite. Another religious leader. He saw the man... and kept walking.

I could've done the same. Maybe I should've.

But I didn't.

I went to him. His face was bruised. His clothes ripped. His eyes barely open.

I cleaned his wounds as best I could with oil and wine. I wrapped him in cloth. I lifted him onto my donkey—every bump in the road making him groan—and I carried him to safety.

At the inn, I stayed with him. Paid for his care. Told the innkeeper to take care of him, no matter the cost.

And you know what? I didn't do it because it made me look good. Or because I thought I'd get a reward.
I did it because... I saw a person who needed help. And I couldn't just look away.
Jesus once asked, *"Which of these was a neighbor to the man who fell among thieves?"*
It wasn't the priest. Or the Levite.
It was me.
Sometimes, your "neighbor" isn't the person who looks like you... or thinks like you... or agrees with you.
Sometimes, being a neighbor means showing compassion when no one else does.

## Reflection Questions:

1. Who in your life might need compassion, even if they're different from you?
2. Have you ever been tempted to "walk by" when someone needed help?
3. What would it look like to be a real neighbor today?

## Prayer:

Dear God,
It's easy to care about people I like... but harder to show love to those who are different. Help me see others the way You do. Give me a heart that shows kindness and compassion—even when it's inconvenient or uncomfortable. Teach me to be a neighbor, like You've called me to be.
Amen.

# Key Verse (KJV):

"Go, and do thou likewise."
— *Luke 10:37b*

# 3. I Buried My Talent — And Regretted It

*(Based on Matthew 25:14–30, KJV — The Parable of the Talents, from the third servant's perspective)*

---

I thought I was being careful.

My master was leaving on a long trip. Before he left, he called us in—three of his servants—and handed out talents. Not talents like singing or drawing... talents as in money. A lot of it.

To one servant, he gave five talents. To another, two. And to me... just one.

I felt small. Unimportant. Like I wasn't trusted with much.

So when the others went off, making deals, taking risks, working hard... I buried mine.

Literally.

I dug a hole in the ground, dropped the talent in, and covered it up. Safe. Hidden. No risk. No way to lose it.

Time passed. The master came back. The first servant? He doubled his five talents—turned them into ten. The second? He did the same with his two.

The master praised them both.

Then came my turn.

I handed him the dirt-covered talent. "Here," I said. "I knew you were strict... I didn't want to mess this up... so I kept it safe."

Safe.

But his face fell.

"You wicked and slothful servant," he said. "You could've at least put it in the bank."

I thought hiding my gift protected me. But really… I wasted it. The truth is, we're all given something. Maybe not money. But gifts. Time. Opportunities. A chance to do something good. And when we bury those things out of fear? We miss the whole point. I thought playing it safe was wise. But I learned the hard way… God calls us to step up, not shrink back.

## Reflection Questions:

1. Have you ever buried your gifts or played it safe because you were afraid to fail?
2. What "talent" or opportunity might God be asking you to use?
3. How can trusting God help you take more bold steps in life?

## Prayer:

Dear God,
Sometimes I hold back because I'm scared—scared to fail, to mess up, to not be enough. But I don't want to bury the things You've given me. Help me to use my gifts with courage. Remind me that You believe in me, and that with You, I can do more than I think.
Amen.

# Key Verse (KJV):

"Well done, thou good and faithful servant... thou hast been faithful over a few things, I will make thee ruler over many things: enter thou into the joy of thy lord."
— *Matthew 25:21*

# 4. I Invested What God Gave Me — And Saw It Grow

*(Based on Matthew 25:14–30, KJV — The Parable of the Talents, from the second servant's perspective)*

⁓⋆⁓

When the master called us together, I didn't expect much. I'm not the smartest. I'm not the boldest. But that day, he entrusted me with two talents. Not as much as the first servant, but still... it was something. It meant he believed in me.

I looked at the coins in my hand. I could've hidden them. Buried them. Played it safe.

But... I didn't want fear to hold me back.

So I invested them.

I bought supplies. I made trades. I took some risks. Some days I doubted myself—wondered if I was messing up—but I kept going. Kept trusting. Kept working.

Little by little... it grew.

By the time the master returned, my two talents had become four.

When it was my turn, I placed them in his hands—nervous, but hopeful.

And his face lit up.

"Well done, thou good and faithful servant," he said. "Thou hast been faithful over a few things, I will make thee ruler over many things."

In that moment, I realized something: it was never about the amount I started with.

It was about what I did with it.

Some people are given five talents. Some two. Some one.

What matters is how we use what God gives us—our gifts, our opportunities, our time.

Playing it safe feels comfortable. But faith? Faith steps out. Faith invests. Faith grows.

## Reflection Questions:

1. What are some "small things" in your life God might want you to be faithful with?
2. Have you ever doubted your abilities because they seemed smaller than someone else's?
3. How can you take a bold step of faith with what God has given you?

## Prayer:

Dear God,
Thank You for trusting me with the gifts You've placed in my life. Even when it feels small, remind me that You can grow it. Help me to be faithful, courageous, and willing to invest in what matters. I want to hear, "Well done" from You. Amen.

## Key Verse (KJV):

"Well done, thou good and faithful servant… thou hast been faithful over a few things, I will make thee ruler over many things: enter thou into the joy of thy lord."
— *Matthew 25:23*

# 5. I Showed Mercy — When It Wasn't Expected

*(Based on Matthew 18:23–35, KJV — The Parable of the Unforgiving Servant, from the first servant's perspective)*

---

I should've been in prison.

I owed the king more money than I could ever repay—millions, really. I messed up. I took more than I should have. I thought I could fix it... but I couldn't.

When the king called me in, I expected the worst. My knees were shaking. My voice cracked as I begged, "Have patience with me... I'll pay it all."

Truthfully? I couldn't. Not in a hundred lifetimes.

But then... he did the unthinkable.

He forgave the debt. Completely. Just like that.

I walked out of there stunned. Free. Lighter than I'd ever felt before.

But then... I saw him.

Another servant. He owed me a small amount—a fraction of what I had owed the king. And suddenly... I forgot what grace felt like. Anger bubbled up. I grabbed him by the shirt.

"Pay me what you owe," I demanded.

He begged, just like I had. But I refused to listen. I had him thrown into prison.

What I didn't realize? The king heard about it.

He called me back in—and this time, his eyes weren't filled with mercy.

"You wicked servant," he said. "I forgave you... shouldn't you have shown mercy, too?"

And just like that... I was thrown into prison.

I had forgotten the most important thing: when you've been forgiven much, you're called to forgive much.

God's mercy isn't meant to stop with me. It's meant to flow through me.

## Reflection Questions:

1. Has someone ever hurt you, and it's been hard to forgive?
2. How does remembering God's forgiveness help you show mercy to others?
3. What's one step you can take toward forgiveness, even if it's hard?

## Prayer:

Dear God,
Sometimes I hold on to anger and forget how much You've forgiven me. Help me to show mercy—even when it's difficult. Remind me that forgiveness sets me free, too. Teach me to love like You love me. Amen.

## Key Verse (KJV):

"Shouldest not thou also have had compassion on thy fellowservant, even as I had pity on thee?"
— *Matthew 18:33*

# 6. I Thought I Deserved More — The Workers in the Vineyard

*(Based on Matthew 20:1–16, KJV — from the perspective of one of the early morning workers)*

---

The work was hard. The sun was brutal. But I was grateful to have a job.

The landowner hired me early that morning. We agreed on the pay—a fair day's wage. I grabbed my tools and got to work in the vineyard.

Hours passed. Sweat dripped. My muscles ached.

Around lunchtime, I noticed more workers arriving. Then again in the afternoon. Even in the last hour before sunset, the landowner brought in more people.

I didn't think much of it... until it was time to get paid.

The ones who only worked an hour? They got the same full-day wage as me.

I blinked. Wait... what?

When it was my turn, I got exactly what we agreed on. But suddenly... it didn't feel fair.

I complained to the landowner. "These guys barely worked! Why do they get the same as me?"

He looked at me—not angry, but firm.

"Didn't we agree on your pay?" he asked. "Is it wrong for me to be generous?"

In that moment, it hit me: I wasn't mad because it was unfair. I was mad because I wanted more.

I thought I deserved better.

But the truth is, God's generosity isn't a competition. His kindness to someone else doesn't take away from me.

Sometimes, I forget that.

Grace isn't about earning. It's about the heart of the One giving it.

## Reflection Questions:

1. Have you ever felt jealous or frustrated when someone else was blessed?
2. Why do you think it's hard to celebrate when others receive kindness?
3. How can you remind yourself that God's love and blessings aren't limited?

## Prayer:

Dear God,
Sometimes I compare myself to others. I want more. I want things to feel "fair." But You remind me that Your generosity is bigger than that. Help me to trust Your timing and be grateful for what You've given me. Amen.

## Key Verse (KJV):

"So the last shall be first, and the first last: for many be called, but few chosen."
— *Matthew 20:16*

# 7. I Built on the Rock — And It Held Firm

*(Based on Matthew 7:24–27, KJV — from the perspective of the wise builder)*

※

Everyone thought I was overthinking it.

When I started building my house, I searched for solid ground.

The easy spots—soft soil, smooth sand—they looked tempting.

Quick. Convenient.

But I kept looking.

I found the rock.

It wasn't easy. The ground was uneven. It took more effort.

More planning. More patience. People shook their heads as they passed by. Some laughed.

Meanwhile, others built on the sand. It was faster. Their houses looked good from the outside—finished long before mine.

But I wasn't worried about how it looked. I was thinking about what was coming.

And sure enough... the storm came.

The wind howled. Rain poured down. The river rose. I watched as the houses built on sand shifted... cracked... collapsed.

But mine? It stood.

The rock held firm.

Jesus once said that everyone who hears His words and follows them is like the wise builder who built on the rock.

That day, I understood what He meant.

It's not about shortcuts. It's not about what looks good to others. It's about building your life on something solid—something that lasts.

And when the storms hit—and they will—it's your foundation that matters most.

## Reflection Questions:

1. What are some "sand" areas you've been tempted to build your life on—things that don't last?
2. How can you make your relationship with God your solid foundation?
3. What choices today will help you stand strong when life gets hard?

## Prayer:

Dear God,
Life can feel shaky sometimes. But I want to build my life on You—the solid Rock that never moves. Help me to trust Your Word, even when it's harder or takes longer. Give me courage to build something strong and lasting with You.
Amen.

## Key Verse (KJV):

"Therefore whosoever heareth these sayings of mine, and doeth them, I will liken him unto a wise man, which built his house upon a rock."
— *Matthew 7:24*

# 8. I Chose the Wide Road — And Got Lost

*(Based on Matthew 7:13–14, KJV — from the perspective of a traveler on the wide road)*

~~~

The wide road looked perfect.

It was paved smooth, wide enough for crowds, and everyone seemed to be going that way. There were signs promising fun, shortcuts, freedom. I didn't even have to think—just follow the crowd.

So I did.

At first, it felt easy. No hills to climb. No tough choices. I blended right in.

But the farther I walked… the more I noticed cracks beneath the surface. Smiles faded. The signs grew confusing. People shoved, tripped, and some even disappeared down side paths.

And then… the end came.

A dead end.

The road that seemed so promising? It led nowhere good.

Empty. Lonely. Lost.

I stood there, heart pounding, realizing I had taken the easy way… and it had cost me.

Then I remembered something I once heard:

"Strait is the gate, and narrow is the way, which leadeth unto life, and few there be that find it."

The narrow road. Harder. Less crowded. But it led somewhere worth going.

So I turned around.

It wasn't easy. The narrow road was rocky, steep, and slow. But with every step, my heart felt lighter. And even though fewer people walked it... I knew where it was leading.

Sometimes, the easy road isn't the best one. The right road? It takes courage to choose... but it's the one that leads home.

## Reflection Questions:

1. Have you ever chosen an easy path in life, only to realize it wasn't the right one?
2. What "wide roads" are tempting you to blend in or take shortcuts?
3. What does walking the narrow road with God look like in your life?

## Prayer:

Dear God,
The wide road is tempting. It feels easy. But I know it doesn't lead to where I want to be. Help me to choose the narrow road—even when it's hard or unpopular. Give me strength to follow You, step by step, all the way home.
Amen.

## Key Verse (KJV):

"Because strait is the gate, and narrow is the way, which leadeth unto life, and few there be that find it."
— *Matthew 7:14*

## 9. I Cared for the Hungry — And Met Jesus There

*(Based on Matthew 25:31–40, KJV — from the perspective of someone surprised to discover they had served Jesus)*

※

I didn't think I'd done anything special.

I wasn't rich. I didn't have power. I wasn't known for making grand gestures. But when I saw someone hungry... I shared my food. When a stranger looked lost... I offered help. When someone was cold... I gave them my spare jacket.

It wasn't a big deal.

At least, that's what I thought.

But then came the day I stood before the King.

I expected judgment, nerves, maybe even regret. But His words stunned me.

"I was hungry, and ye gave me meat. I was thirsty, and ye gave me drink. I was a stranger, and ye took me in."

I blinked. What? When?

I had never seen Him before—never served Him directly.

So I asked, "Lord, when did we see You hungry, or thirsty, or a stranger?"

He smiled. "Inasmuch as ye have done it unto one of the least of these... ye have done it unto me."

Suddenly, every small act of kindness flooded my mind—the simple, ordinary moments I barely remembered.

Turns out… those moments weren't ordinary at all.

Every time I cared for someone in need… I was caring for Him.

I didn't have to be perfect. I didn't have to be noticed. I just had to love.

And Jesus noticed that.

## Reflection Questions:

1. Have you ever overlooked small opportunities to help someone because they seemed unimportant?
2. How does knowing Jesus sees those moments change the way you treat others?
3. What's one simple way you can show kindness or serve someone this week?

## Prayer:

Dear Jesus,
Thank You for reminding me that You see even the smallest acts of love. Help me to care for others with a willing heart—not for attention, but because it matters to You. Show me the people around me who need kindness, and help me love them like You do.
Amen.

## Key Verse (KJV):

"Inasmuch as ye have done it unto one of the least of these my brethren, ye have done it unto me."
— *Matthew 25:40b*

# 10. I Let My Light Shine — Even When It Felt Small

*(Based on Matthew 5:14–16, KJV — from the perspective of someone discovering the impact of their small light)*

---

I used to think my light didn't matter.

There were so many people brighter, louder, stronger. I figured I could just blend in... stay quiet... stay safe.

But Jesus had different plans.

"You are the light of the world," He said. "A city set on a hill cannot be hid."

At first, I wanted to hide. It felt easier. Who notices one small candle, anyway?

But I couldn't shake His words.

So... I tried.

It wasn't perfect. I offered encouragement when someone was hurting. I stood up for a classmate when others were silent. I stayed kind when it would've been easier to join in the jokes.

Small things.

But something happened.

Little by little, people noticed. Not because I was trying to impress them—but because the light inside me? It pointed to something... Someone... bigger than me.

Jesus.

The world is dark sometimes. People feel lost, forgotten, overwhelmed.

But a little light? It makes all the difference.

And the truth is... when we hide our light, we don't just lose our courage—we keep others from seeing hope.

I may not be the brightest. But I'm not hiding anymore.

Because even a small light can lead someone home.

## Reflection Questions:

1. Have you ever felt like your faith or kindness wasn't enough to make a difference?
2. What keeps you from letting your light shine for others to see?
3. How can you reflect Jesus in small but powerful ways this week?

## Prayer:

Dear God,
Sometimes I feel small—like my words or actions don't matter. But You remind me that even a little light can change the darkness. Help me to be bold, to be kind, and to let my life reflect Your love. Use my small light to bring hope to the world.
Amen.

## Key Verse (KJV):

"Let your light so shine before men, that they may see your good works, and glorify your Father which is in heaven."
— *Matthew 5:16*

## 11. I Almost Missed the Banquet — But I Said Yes

*(Based on Luke 14:15–24, KJV — from the perspective of one of the last-minute guests at the great banquet)*

---

I never expected an invitation like that.

The banquet was for important people. The rich. The powerful. People who mattered.

I didn't exactly fit that description.

So when the servant came running down my street, telling me the master wanted me at his feast, I froze.

"Me?" I asked, pointing to myself.

"Yeah, you," he smiled. "The others made excuses. They were too busy. Too proud. But the master? He wants the house full."

I couldn't believe it.

I'd seen that house before—its tall gates, its grand halls, the smell of food drifting through the windows.

And now... I was invited inside.

I almost said no. It felt too good to be true. Maybe I didn't deserve it. Maybe I wasn't dressed right. But deep down, I knew... I couldn't miss this.

So I said yes.

And when I walked through those doors, the table stretched farther than I could see. Plates overflowing. Music playing. Laughter filling the room.

The master looked at me—and smiled.

Jesus once told this story to remind us: God invites everyone.

But not everyone accepts.

Some are too distracted. Some feel unworthy. But those who say yes? They discover a seat at His table.

I almost missed it. But I'm glad I didn't.

## Reflection Questions:

1. Have you ever felt like you weren't "good enough" for God's invitation?
2. What distractions or excuses sometimes keep you from saying yes to Him?
3. How can you accept—and enjoy—the invitation God offers today?

## Prayer:

Dear God,
Thank You for inviting me—even when I feel unworthy or unsure. Help me not to miss the opportunities You place in front of me. Give me courage to say yes to You, to walk through the doors You open, and to enjoy the life You're offering.
Amen.

## Key Verse (KJV):

"For I say unto you, That none of those men which were bidden shall taste of my supper."
— *Luke 14:24*

## 12. I Refused the Invitation — And Missed Everything

*(Based on Luke 14:15–24, KJV — from the perspective of one of the invited guests who made excuses)*

―――

I had every intention of going.

When the invitation to the banquet arrived, I was flattered. It was from the master himself—the richest, most respected man in town. His parties were legendary.

But... life got busy.

I had just bought some land. It needed my attention. I told myself, *It's not like the banquet's going anywhere.*

Another guest bought oxen—business to run, money to make.

Someone else got married—family responsibilities.

One by one, we made our excuses. I even rehearsed mine, tried to make it sound convincing:

"Please have me excused. I really want to come... just not today."

What I didn't realize? That was my only chance.

The master heard our excuses—and he was done waiting.

He sent his servant into the streets. The poor. The outsiders. The forgotten. They filled the banquet hall.

And me? I missed it.

The doors closed. The music played. The feast went on... without me.

Jesus told this story to show how easy it is to say no to God—not with anger, but with distractions. With busyness. With "not now."

I thought I could delay the invitation. But I missed everything.

## Reflection Questions:

1. What distractions or responsibilities sometimes pull you away from spending time with God?
2. Have you ever told God "not now" with your actions, even if you didn't say the words?
3. What would it look like to make God's invitation a priority today?

## Prayer:

Dear God,
It's easy to make excuses. Life feels busy, and sometimes I put You last. But I don't want to miss what You have for me. Help me to say yes—to Your love, to Your plans, to the life You're inviting me into.
Amen.

## Key Verse (KJV):

"And they all with one consent began to make excuse."
— *Luke 14:18a*

## 13. I Waited for the Bridegroom — And I Was Ready

*(Based on Matthew 25:1–13, KJV — from the perspective of one of the wise bridesmaids)*

―❦―

We didn't know when he was coming.

The bridegroom's arrival was always unpredictable—maybe tonight, maybe tomorrow. But when you're part of the wedding party, you wait. That's how it works.

So, we prepared.

I made sure I had my lamp and plenty of oil. It might sound boring, but I'd seen what happens to those who aren't ready.

The night dragged on. The stars stretched across the sky. Some of the others started yawning. A few nodded off.

Suddenly—shouts echoed in the street.

"He's coming! The bridegroom is coming!"

We jumped to our feet. I grabbed my lamp, trimmed the wick, and lit it. It shone bright and steady.

But not everyone was ready.

The others fumbled with empty lamps. "Share your oil!" they begged.

But I couldn't. It wasn't selfish—it was reality. You can't borrow someone else's preparation.

They ran off to find oil. Meanwhile, the bridegroom arrived. We followed him inside. The doors closed behind us.

The celebration began.

The others came later... too late.

Jesus told this story to remind us: faith isn't about scrambling at the last second. It's about being ready—living ready.

I didn't have all the answers. But I had my lamp... and I was ready.

## Reflection Questions:

1. What does "being ready" for Jesus look like in your everyday life?
2. Have you ever procrastinated with something important and regretted it?
3. How can you stay prepared spiritually, even when life feels ordinary?

## Prayer:

Dear God,
I don't always feel ready. But I want to live prepared—to love You, follow You, and stay faithful even when it feels like nothing's happening. Help me to be like the wise bridesmaids—to carry my light, to stay watchful, and to be ready when You call.
Amen.

## Key Verse (KJV):

"Watch therefore, for ye know neither the day nor the hour wherein the Son of man cometh."
— *Matthew 25:13*

## 14. I Ran Out of Oil — And Missed the Door

*(Based on Matthew 25:1–13, KJV — from the perspective of one of the foolish bridesmaids)*

I thought I had more time.

The bridegroom's arrival was always unpredictable. We all knew that. But honestly? I didn't think it mattered that much.

I had my lamp. That felt like enough.

But I didn't bring extra oil.

The night dragged on. We waited. The others—some of them—kept checking their supplies, making sure they were prepared.

Me? I got comfortable. Closed my eyes for a bit. Told myself I'd deal with it later.

Then the shout came:

"He's here! The bridegroom is coming!"

Panic hit me like a wave.

I grabbed my lamp. It flickered... sputtered... died.

I turned to the others. "Share your oil!" I begged.

But they couldn't. Their preparation wasn't mine to borrow.

I ran to buy more. Rushed back. But by the time I returned... the door was closed.

I knocked. I pleaded. But it was too late.

Jesus told this story to remind us: some things can't be rushed. You can't fake readiness. You can't borrow faith.

I thought I had more time.

But I missed the door.

## Reflection Questions:

1. Have you ever assumed you had more time to get serious about your faith?
2. What "oil" (spiritual preparation) do you need to be building up in your life?
3. How can you live ready for Jesus today, not someday?

## Prayer:

Dear God,
I've let distractions and excuses make me think I have all the time in the world. But You remind me that some moments won't wait. Help me to stay ready—not out of fear, but because I want to know You. Teach me to live prepared, so I never miss the door.
Amen.

## Key Verse (KJV):

"And while they went to buy, the bridegroom came; and they that were ready went in with him... and the door was shut."
— *Matthew 25:10*

# 15. I Forgave My Debtor — Because I'd Been Forgiven

*(Based on Matthew 18:23–35, KJV — from the perspective of the second servant who was forgiven by his fellow servant)*

---

I owed him money. Not much—but enough to keep me up at night.

Life had been hard lately. Work was slow. Bills stacked up. And the debt? It hung over me like a cloud.

Then one day, it happened.

The man I owed found me.

My heart sank. I expected anger. Demands. Maybe even threats. But... he didn't yell. His eyes softened. He told me a story—about how the king had forgiven him. Completely. A debt way bigger than mine.

And because of that? He forgave me.

Just like that.

I could barely speak. Relief, gratitude, disbelief—all tangled together.

I didn't deserve his mercy. But I got it anyway.

And you know what? That moment changed me.

It made me realize how easy it is to hold grudges... to demand payback... to cling to bitterness.

But when you've been forgiven? Truly forgiven? It humbles you. Softens you.

I don't want to live with clenched fists and a hard heart.
I want to live like someone who knows what mercy feels like—
and passes it on.

## Reflection Questions:

1. Have you ever experienced forgiveness from someone that changed your perspective?
2. Why do you think it's so hard to forgive others, even when we've been forgiven?
3. How can you practice showing mercy to others, like God has shown to you?

## Prayer:

Dear God,
You've forgiven me more than I deserve. Help me not to forget that. When I'm tempted to hold on to anger or demand payback, remind me of Your mercy. Teach me to live with an open heart—and to forgive like You forgive me.
Amen.

## Key Verse (KJV):

"Shouldest not thou also have had compassion on thy fellowservant, even as I had pity on thee?"
— *Matthew 18:33*

# 16. I Refused to Forgive — And Paid the Price

*(Based on Matthew 18:23–35, KJV — from the perspective of the unforgiving servant)*

---

I never thought the king would actually forgive me.

My debt was huge. Impossible to repay. I deserved punishment.

But when I begged for mercy... the king did the unthinkable.

He cancelled my debt. Just like that.

I walked out of the palace lighter than air. Free. Clear. It should've changed me.

But it didn't.

The first person I saw? A fellow servant who owed me money.

Compared to my debt, his was nothing.

But all I could think about was what he owed me. The power I had now.

So I grabbed him. Shouted. Demanded repayment. He pleaded, just like I had.

But I wasn't interested in mercy.

I had him thrown into prison.

It felt good... for a moment.

Until word got back to the king.

He called me back in. His eyes weren't filled with compassion this time.

"You wicked servant," he said. "I forgave you... shouldn't you have shown mercy too?"

I had no answer.

The forgiveness I'd been given? I threw it away by refusing to give it to someone else.

And now... I was the one behind bars.

Jesus told this story to show that unforgiveness doesn't just hurt others—it traps you, too.

I learned that the hard way.

## Reflection Questions:

1. Have you ever held on to anger or bitterness, even when you've experienced forgiveness?
2. Why do you think it's so hard to show mercy when we feel wronged?
3. How does unforgiveness affect your heart and your relationship with God?

## Prayer:

Dear God,
It's hard to let go when I've been hurt. But I don't want to live stuck in bitterness. You've forgiven me more than I can ever repay. Help me to forgive others—even when it's hard. Teach me to show the same mercy You've shown me.
Amen.

## Key Verse (KJV):

"Shouldest not thou also have had compassion on thy fellowservant, even as I had pity on thee?"
— *Matthew 18:33*

# 17. I Found the Pearl of Great Price — And Let Go of the Rest

*(Based on Matthew 13:45–46, KJV — from the perspective of the merchant searching for pearls)*

༄

I've always been a seeker.

As a merchant, I spent my life searching for treasure—fine jewels, rare pearls, things worth showing off and selling for profit.

I've seen it all. But nothing prepared me for that day.

I was walking through the market when I saw it.

The pearl.

Perfect. Smooth. Radiant. The kind of beauty you only dream of finding. One glance, and I knew—it was worth more than everything I owned.

But there was a cost.

To have it, I had to give up everything else.

My coins. My shop. Every other pearl I'd collected along the way.

It wasn't an easy decision. But I couldn't walk away.

So, I sold it all.

People thought I was crazy. But when I held that pearl in my hand, I knew I'd made the right choice.

Jesus said the kingdom of heaven is like that pearl.

It's more valuable than money, success, or comfort. But it costs something—it means letting go of what we think matters most.
I could've clung to the ordinary.
But I chose the extraordinary.
And I've never regretted it.

## Reflection Questions:

1. What are some things in your life that feel valuable but might be keeping you from fully following God?
2. Why do you think letting go of some things is necessary to experience God's best?
3. What would it look like to seek God's kingdom first in your life?

## Prayer:

Dear God,
I want what You have for me—even if it means letting go of the things I cling to. Help me to see the true value of Your kingdom. Teach me to give up the ordinary for the extraordinary life You're offering.
Amen.

## Key Verse (KJV):

"Who, when he had found one pearl of great price, went and sold all that he had, and bought it."
— *Matthew 13:46*

## 18. I Discovered Treasure in the Field — And Everything Changed

*(Based on Matthew 13:44, KJV — from the perspective of the man who found hidden treasure in a field)*

---

I wasn't looking for treasure.

It was just another ordinary day, working in the fields. Dirt under my nails. Sweat on my face. Same routine as always.

But then... my shovel hit something hard.

Curious, I dug deeper. And that's when I saw it.

A chest.

I opened it—and my heart nearly stopped.

Treasure.

Gold. Jewels. Wealth beyond anything I'd ever imagined.

It wasn't mine—not yet. But it could be.

I covered it back up. My hands trembled with excitement as I raced home.

I sold everything. My house. My tools. Even the clothes on my back if I had to.

People called me crazy. They didn't know.

They didn't see the treasure I saw.

When I had enough, I bought that field.

And the treasure? It was mine.

Jesus said the kingdom of heaven is like that treasure.

At first, it looks hidden. Ordinary. Easy to overlook.

But when you discover it... when you truly see what God offers... it changes everything.

You'll give up anything to have it.

And it's worth it.

## Reflection Questions:

1. Have you ever overlooked the value of your relationship with God in daily life?
2. What might you need to let go of to fully experience the treasure of God's kingdom?
3. How can you remind yourself that faith is the greatest treasure you'll ever find?

## Prayer:

Dear God,
Sometimes I forget how valuable Your kingdom really is. I get distracted by things that don't last. Help me to see the treasure You've placed in front of me. Teach me to let go of anything holding me back and to choose You above all else.
Amen.

## Key Verse (KJV):

"Again, the kingdom of heaven is like unto treasure hid in a field; the which when a man hath found, he hideth... and buyeth that field."
— *Matthew 13:44*

## 19. I Cast My Net — And God Filled It

*(Based on Matthew 13:47–50, KJV — from the perspective of a fisherman in the parable of the net)*

---

Fishing is in my blood.

It's not glamorous. It's hard work. You cast the net. You haul it in. Over and over again.

Most days, it feels ordinary. Routine.

But that day? It was different.

We cast the net like always. But when we pulled it back in... it was overflowing.

Fish of every kind—big, small, good, bad—all tangled together.

We couldn't keep them all. Some were good for keeping. Others... we tossed back into the sea.

Jesus explained it later.

"The kingdom of heaven is like a net cast into the sea," He said. "At the end, the good will be gathered in, and the bad cast away."

At first, it sounded harsh. But the more I thought about it, the more it made sense.

Not everyone who hears about God chooses Him. Some stay tangled in selfishness, pride, or fear.

But those who follow Him? Those who let their hearts be caught by His love?

They're gathered in. Kept close.

That net? It reminded me that God's invitation goes out to everyone.

But in the end… we choose whether we stay.

## Reflection Questions:

1. What does it mean to you that God invites everyone into His kingdom?
2. How do your daily choices show whether you're following God or drifting away?
3. What would it look like to let God "catch" your heart completely?

## Prayer:

Dear God,
Thank You for casting Your net wide—for inviting everyone, including me. Help me to be one of those who stays close, who follows You, and who chooses to live for You every day. Catch my heart, God, and don't let me drift away.
Amen.

## Key Verse (KJV):

"Again, the kingdom of heaven is like unto a net, that was cast into the sea, and gathered of every kind."
— *Matthew 13:47*

## 20. I Lost One Sheep — And Searched Until I Found It

*(Based on Luke 15:3–7, KJV — from the perspective of the shepherd in the parable of the lost sheep)*

---

Ninety-nine sheep is a good number.

It means your flock is thriving. It means you're doing your job right.

But when I counted them that day… only ninety-nine were there.

One was missing.

Some shepherds might've shrugged it off. "It's just one," they'd say. "Not worth the trouble."

But not me.

Every sheep matters. Even one.

So, I left the ninety-nine in the safety of the fold and set off into the wilderness.

The hills were steep. The thorns scratched my arms. The rocks scraped my knees.

But I kept going.

I called out. I searched high and low.

And finally… I found him.

Tangled in the bushes. Shivering. Scared.

I didn't scold him. I didn't push him along. I picked him up, carried him home, and celebrated.

Jesus said that's exactly what heaven is like when one lost person finds their way back to God.

The world may write you off. You may feel small, forgotten, replaceable.

But to God? You are worth searching for.

And He won't stop... until He finds you.

## Reflection Questions:

1. Have you ever felt like you've wandered away from God or gotten lost spiritually?
2. How does it feel knowing God searches for you and never gives up?
3. How can you remind someone else they are worth being found?

## Prayer:

Dear God,
Sometimes I wander. I lose my way. But You never stop searching for me. Thank You for loving me enough to come after me. Help me to stay close to You—and remind me that I'm never forgotten.
Amen.

## Key Verse (KJV):

"And when he hath found it, he layeth it on his shoulders, rejoicing."
— *Luke 15:5*

## 21. I Was the Lost Coin — But I Was Never Forgotten

*(Based on Luke 15:8–10, KJV — from the perspective of the lost coin in the parable)*

❦

I didn't mean to get lost.

One moment, I was safe among the other coins. Part of something valuable. Seen. Counted.

Then... gone.

I slipped through the cracks, hidden in the dust and shadows. Days passed. Maybe longer. It felt like no one noticed. No one cared. I was small. Insignificant.

Or so I thought.

But she cared.

The woman who owned me? She turned the house upside down looking for me. She lit a lamp, swept every corner, searched under every rug.

She wouldn't stop.

It felt impossible. But finally... her hand brushed against me. She lifted me up—dusty, forgotten... but still hers.

And she celebrated.

It may sound silly—a party for finding a coin—but Jesus said that's exactly what happens in heaven when one person turns back to God.

You may feel small. You may feel overlooked.

But you're never forgotten.

God sees. God searches. And when you're found... all of heaven celebrates.

## Reflection Questions:

1. Have you ever felt overlooked, lost, or insignificant?
2. How does it feel knowing God notices and values you, even when you feel hidden?
3. What does it mean to "be found" by God in your life right now?

## Prayer:

Dear God,
Sometimes I feel small or forgotten. But You remind me I'm valuable to You. Thank You for never giving up on me, for searching for me, and for celebrating when I'm close to You. Help me to believe that I matter—always.
Amen.

## Key Verse (KJV):

"Likewise, I say unto you, there is joy in the presence of the angels of God over one sinner that repenteth."
— *Luke 15:10*

## 22. I Was a Mustard Seed — Small, But Growing

*(Based on Matthew 13:31–32, KJV — from the perspective of the mustard seed in the parable)*

---

I've always been small.

Easily overlooked. Easily forgotten. People toss me aside, barely noticing.

Other seeds? They get all the attention—big, flashy, promising.

But not me.

I'm just... tiny.

But buried in the soil, hidden in the dark, something unexpected happened.

I began to grow.

Slow at first. A sprout. Then leaves. Then branches stretching toward the sky.

Day by day, I kept pushing through the dirt, reaching higher, digging deeper.

It wasn't overnight. It wasn't easy.

But eventually... I became more than anyone expected.

A tree.

Birds came to rest in my branches. People found shade beneath me. I became a home, a shelter, a sign of hope.

Jesus said the kingdom of heaven is like me—a mustard seed.

Small at first. Easy to underestimate.

But give it time... and it grows beyond what anyone imagined.

Maybe you feel small. Overlooked. Like your faith doesn't make a difference.

But small doesn't mean weak.

Small doesn't mean stuck.

God takes small things—and grows them into something amazing.

## Reflection Questions:

1. Have you ever felt small or insignificant in your faith or life?
2. What are some "small seeds" of faith or kindness you can plant today?
3. How can you trust that God is growing something in you, even when you don't see it yet?

## Prayer:

Dear God,
Sometimes I feel small, like my faith or efforts don't matter. But You remind me that even tiny seeds can grow into something great. Help me to trust the process. Grow something strong and beautiful in me for Your glory.
Amen.

## Key Verse (KJV):

"The kingdom of heaven is like to a grain of mustard seed... which indeed is the least of all seeds: but when it is grown... it becometh a tree."
— *Matthew 13:31–32 (selected)*

# 23. I Was Yeast in the Dough — And God Used Me

*(Based on Matthew 13:33, KJV — from the perspective of the yeast in the parable)*

---

I wasn't impressive.

Just a pinch of yeast. Tiny. Ordinary. Most people don't even notice me.

But once I'm mixed into the dough... everything changes.

At first, it doesn't seem like much is happening. The flour, the water, the salt—it all looks the same.

But quietly... I get to work.

I spread through every corner of the dough. Slowly. Steadily. Making it rise. Expanding it. Transforming it.

Before long, that lump of dough doubles in size—soft, ready, full of life.

Jesus said the kingdom of heaven is like me—yeast hidden in the dough.

You may not always see the difference faith makes right away.

But trust me... it's happening.

Your kindness. Your prayers. Your quiet choices to follow God when no one's watching.

They rise.

They grow.

They change everything.

I may be small.

But in the right hands... I make an impact that can't be missed.

## Reflection Questions:

1. Have you ever felt like your faith or influence is too small to matter?
2. What quiet, behind-the-scenes ways can you live out your faith?
3. How does this parable encourage you to keep trusting that small things grow?

## Prayer:

Dear God,
I want to be like that yeast—small, but making a difference. Remind me that I don't have to be loud or seen to help Your kingdom grow. Help my life quietly influence the world around me for You.
Amen.

## Key Verse (KJV):

"The kingdom of heaven is like unto leaven, which a woman took, and hid in three measures of meal, till the whole was leavened."
— *Matthew 13:33*

## 24. I Knocked — And the Door Opened

*(Based on Luke 11:5–10, KJV — from the perspective of the friend knocking at midnight)*

❦

It was late. Way past bedtime.

But I couldn't stay home. I had a friend visiting—unexpected, hungry, tired—and I had nothing to offer him.

So, I grabbed my cloak and headed out into the night.

I stood at my neighbor's door and knocked.

Nothing.

I knocked again. Harder.

Finally, a groggy voice called from inside. "What do you want? It's midnight! We're already in bed."

I hesitated. It felt awkward. But I couldn't turn back empty-handed.

So, I kept knocking.

Louder this time.

I heard sighs. The shuffle of feet. Then... the door creaked open. Without another word, he handed me what I needed—bread for my friend.

Jesus told this story to remind us that sometimes, you have to keep asking. Keep seeking. Keep knocking.

God doesn't get annoyed with our persistence. He welcomes it.

When we knock in prayer, with faith, the door opens.

Maybe not always in the way we expect.

But it opens.

## Reflection Questions:

1. Have you ever prayed for something but felt like giving up?
2. What does this story teach you about persistence with God?
3. How can you remind yourself to keep knocking, even when answers feel delayed?

## Prayer:

Dear God,
Sometimes I feel like You're not listening, like the door is closed. But You remind me to keep asking, to keep knocking, to keep trusting. Help me not to give up in prayer. I believe You hear me—and I trust that the door will open in Your perfect time. Amen.

## Key Verse (KJV):

"For every one that asketh receiveth; and he that seeketh findeth; and to him that knocketh it shall be opened."
— *Luke 11:10*

## 25. I Asked — And He Answered

*(Based on Matthew 7:7–11, KJV — from the perspective of someone learning to trust in asking God)*

---

I used to think asking wasn't worth it.

What if the answer was no? What if I looked weak? What if God didn't care?

So, I stayed quiet. I tried to figure life out on my own.

But it got exhausting—carrying burdens I wasn't meant to carry, trying to fix problems that were bigger than me.

Then I remembered what Jesus said.

"Ask, and it shall be given you. Seek, and ye shall find. Knock, and it shall be opened unto you."

It sounded simple. Almost too simple.

But I tried.

I prayed—not fancy, not perfect. Just honest.

God, I need You. I need help. I can't do this alone.

At first, I wasn't sure anything changed.

But little by little, I saw it.

The strength to face the day. The courage to take a hard step.

The peace that didn't make sense.

I asked—and He answered.

Not always the way I expected.

But He heard me.

And He hears you, too.

## Reflection Questions:

1. Have you ever hesitated to ask God for help, feeling unsure if He cares?
2. How does Jesus' promise encourage you to bring your needs to God?
3. What's one thing you need to ask God for today with honest faith?

## Prayer:

Dear God,
Thank You for being the kind of Father who listens. Sometimes I feel silly or scared to ask, but You remind me that You care about every part of my life. Help me to ask boldly, trust fully, and believe that You hear me.
Amen.

## Key Verse (KJV):

"Ask, and it shall be given you; seek, and ye shall find; knock, and it shall be opened unto you."
— *Matthew 7:7*

## 26. I Kept Praying — And God Heard Me

*(Based on Luke 18:1–8, KJV — from the perspective of the persistent widow in the parable)*

---

People told me to give up.

They said the judge didn't care. That he was too powerful. That no one could change his mind.

But I couldn't stop.

I had been wronged—treated unfairly. And no one else seemed to care.

So I went to the judge. Again and again.

He ignored me. Rolled his eyes. Shut the door in my face.

But I kept going.

Day after day.

Week after week.

Until finally... he cracked.

"Because this widow troubleth me, I will avenge her," he said.

Justice. At last.

Jesus told this story to remind us that if even an unjust judge listens eventually... how much more will God—the loving, perfect Judge—hear us when we pray?

It doesn't always happen overnight. Sometimes, it feels like silence.

But when you keep praying? When you keep trusting?

God hears.

And He answers.

## Reflection Questions:

1. Have you ever felt like your prayers weren't being heard?
2. What keeps you from giving up when you're waiting on God?
3. How can you be persistent in prayer while still trusting God's timing?

## Prayer:

Dear God,
Sometimes I feel discouraged when I pray and don't see answers right away. But You remind me to keep going. To keep asking. To keep trusting. Give me the faith to be persistent and the patience to believe You're always working behind the scenes. Amen.

## Key Verse (KJV):

"And shall not God avenge his own elect, which cry day and night unto him... I tell you that he will avenge them speedily."
— *Luke 18:7–8a*

# 27. I Gave a Cup of Water — And It Mattered

*(Based on Matthew 10:42, KJV — from the perspective of someone who showed simple kindness in Jesus' name)*

---

It didn't seem like much.

Just a cup of water.

The traveler looked exhausted. Dust clung to his clothes. His face was flushed from the heat.

I almost walked past him. Someone else could help. Someone more important.

But something stirred in me.

So, I filled a cup with cool water and handed it to him.

His eyes lit up with surprise. Gratitude.

It was a small thing. Barely worth mentioning.

But later, I remembered what Jesus had said:

"Whosoever shall give to drink unto one of these little ones… a cup of cold water only… shall in no wise lose his reward."

It hit me.

In God's eyes, small things matter.

A cup of water.

A kind word.

A quiet prayer.

They may feel invisible to the world.

But God sees.

And He promises that nothing done in His name is ever wasted.

Even a simple cup of water can ripple into eternity.

## Reflection Questions:

1. Have you ever doubted that small acts of kindness really matter?
2. What's one small, practical way you can serve someone today?
3. How does this story change the way you think about simple, unnoticed actions?

## Prayer:

Dear God,
Thank You for reminding me that little things make a big difference. Help me not to overlook opportunities to show kindness, even in small ways. Teach me to serve others with love, knowing that You see and that it matters to You.
Amen.

## Key Verse (KJV):

"And whosoever shall give to drink unto one of these little ones a cup of cold water... verily I say unto you, he shall in no wise lose his reward."
— *Matthew 10:42*

## 28. I Heard the Wise Builder's Warning — And Changed Course

*(Based on Matthew 7:24–27, KJV — from the perspective of someone who almost built on sand)*

―※―

I almost made the mistake.

The beach looked perfect—smooth, wide, easy to build on. The sand was soft beneath my feet. It would've been quick, convenient, impressive.

But then... I heard the wise builder's warning.

He'd been through storms before. He knew the danger.

"Sand shifts," he said. "When the rain falls and the wind blows, everything falls apart."

I didn't want to believe him at first. The sand looked fine.

But deep down, I knew... he was right.

So, I chose differently.

I found solid ground—rock beneath my foundation. It took more effort. More patience. More digging. But when the storm came—and it did—my house stood firm.

Jesus said those who hear His words and follow them are like the wise builder.

The storms of life? They're coming.

But when your foundation is faith, not feelings... obedience, not convenience... you stand.

I almost built on sand.

But I'm glad I listened.

## Reflection Questions:

1. What "sand" (unstable foundations) are you tempted to build your life on?
2. How can you build your life on God's truth, even when it's harder or takes longer?
3. What choices today will help your faith stand strong when life gets tough?

## Prayer:

Dear God,
I don't want to build my life on things that won't last. Teach me to listen to Your wisdom, even when it's not the easy way. Help me build on the solid rock of Your truth, so I can stand strong no matter what storms come.
Amen.

## Key Verse (KJV):

"Therefore whosoever heareth these sayings of mine, and doeth them, I will liken him unto a wise man, which built his house upon a rock."
— *Matthew 7:24*

## 29. I Hid My Lamp — But the Darkness Grew

*(Based on Luke 8:16, KJV — from the perspective of someone who hid their light)*

❦

At first, I thought I was being smart.

I had my lamp—my little flame of faith—but I kept it hidden.

Why?

Because standing out felt risky.

Because people might judge me.

Because the darkness was everywhere, and it felt safer to blend in.

So, I covered my light.

No one saw it.

No one asked questions.

No one criticized me.

But the darkness?

It stayed.

It grew.

People stumbled. They searched for direction. They needed light... and I had it.

But I hid it.

Jesus said no one lights a lamp and hides it under a vessel. It defeats the purpose.

Light is meant to shine.

And faith? It's meant to be seen.

I realized that hiding my light didn't protect me... it just robbed others of hope.

So, I uncovered it.

It wasn't the biggest or brightest. But in the dark? Even a small flame makes a difference.

And together? Our lights push back the dark.

## Reflection Questions:

1. Have you ever hidden your faith because you were afraid of what others might think?
2. What does it look like to let your light shine, even in small ways?
3. How can your faith encourage someone else who feels lost in the dark?

## Prayer:

Dear God,
Forgive me for hiding my faith when I should've shared it. Give me courage to shine, even when it feels scary. Help me to remember that even a small light can push back the darkness—and that You're always with me.
Amen.

## Key Verse (KJV):

"No man, when he hath lighted a candle, covereth it with a vessel... but setteth it on a candlestick, that they which enter in may see the light."
— *Luke 8:16*

# 30. I Shined My Light — And It Reached Others

*(Based on Matthew 5:14–16, KJV — from the perspective of someone who chose to let their light shine)*

---

For a long time, I thought my light didn't matter.

I wasn't loud. I wasn't famous. I wasn't the type people looked up to.

But then I remembered what Jesus said:

"You are the light of the world."

Not the biggest. Not the brightest. But still... light.

So, I decided to stop hiding.

I let my kindness show, even when others weren't kind.

I stood up for the quiet kid, even when it felt awkward.

I shared my faith, even when my voice shook.

At first, it felt small. But little by little, people noticed.

The kid I helped? He smiled for the first time in weeks.

The friend I encouraged? She asked about my faith.

The person who saw me standing up? They found courage to do the same.

It wasn't about being perfect or impressive.

It was about shining.

Jesus didn't say, "Be the biggest light." He said, "Let your light shine."

In the dark, even a little light reaches far.

I finally stopped hiding mine.

And it made more of a difference than I ever expected.

**Reflection Questions:**
1. What fears hold you back from letting your light shine?
2. How can your actions or words reflect God's love in your everyday life?
3. Who in your life might need your light right now?

## Prayer:

Dear God,
Thank You for giving me a light to shine. Even when I feel small or scared, remind me that You can use me. Help me to be bold, to be kind, and to reflect Your love in every situation. Let my light make a difference.
Amen.

## Key Verse (KJV):

"Let your light so shine before men, that they may see your good works, and glorify your Father which is in heaven."
— *Matthew 5:16*

## 31. I Came Empty — But God Filled Me

*(Based on Luke 14:15–24, KJV — from the perspective of one of the unexpected guests at the great banquet)*

---

I didn't belong at the banquet.

The grand house? The fancy table? The feast? It wasn't meant for people like me.

I had no invitation. No status. No fancy clothes.

But the servant came to me anyway.

"The master sent me," he said. "The ones who were invited… they're too busy. But you? You're invited now."

I hesitated. I had nothing to bring. Nothing to offer. But deep down, I knew… I couldn't miss this.

So, I came.

I walked through the grand doors, feeling awkward and underdressed. But no one looked down on me. The master smiled. The room was full of people just like me—unexpected guests. Unlikely guests.

We came empty.

But we left full.

Jesus told this story to remind us that God invites everyone—especially those who feel unworthy.

It's not about what you bring.

It's about showing up.

I came empty.

But God filled me with more than I ever imagined.

## Reflection Questions:

1. Have you ever felt like you didn't belong or weren't "good enough" for God's love?
2. What keeps you from accepting God's invitation in your life?
3. How does this story remind you that God welcomes everyone—including you?

## Prayer:

Dear God,
Sometimes I feel like I don't belong. But You remind me that Your invitation is for everyone—including me. Help me to come to You, even when I feel empty. Thank You for filling me with Your love, Your grace, and Your purpose.
Amen.

## Key Verse (KJV):

"Go out into the highways and hedges, and compel them to come in, that my house may be filled."
— *Luke 14:23*

## 32. I Thought I Was Too Late — But God Was Patient

*(Based on Matthew 20:1–16, KJV — from the perspective of the late-day worker in the vineyard)*

---

I thought I'd missed my chance.

All day, I waited in the marketplace, hoping someone would hire me. But as the sun climbed higher, my hope sank lower.

By noon... nothing.

By afternoon... nothing.

By the final hour, I was ready to give up.

Then the landowner came.

"Why stand ye here all the day idle?" he asked.

I shrugged. "No one's hired me."

"Come," he said. "There's still work to do."

I didn't expect much. An hour's pay, maybe. But I was grateful for anything.

When the day ended, he paid the workers.

Those who started early? They got a full day's wage.

And me? I braced for less... but to my shock, I received the same.

The others grumbled. "It's not fair," they said.

But the landowner reminded them:

"My generosity isn't about fairness—it's about kindness."

Jesus told this story to remind us that with God, it's never too late to start.

No matter when you come to Him... He welcomes you.

I thought I'd missed my chance.

But God was patient.

And His grace? It's for all of us.

## Reflection Questions:

1. Have you ever felt like it's too late to grow in your faith or change your life?
2. What does this story teach you about God's patience and generosity?
3. How can you trust that God welcomes you, no matter when you come to Him?

## Prayer:

Dear God,
Thank You for being patient with me. Even when I feel late, lost, or behind, You remind me that Your love and grace are always available. Help me not to compare myself to others, but to simply say yes to You—right now.
Amen.

## Key Verse (KJV):

"So the last shall be first, and the first last: for many be called, but few chosen."
— *Matthew 20:16*

## 33. I Was a Stubborn Soil — But God Kept Planting

*(Based on Matthew 13:3–9, 18–23, KJV — from the perspective of the soil in the parable of the sower)*

❦

I didn't think I was the problem.

The seeds kept landing... but they never grew.

At first, I blamed the birds—they snatched the seeds away.

Then the sun—too hot, too harsh.

Then the weeds—choking everything that tried to sprout.

But deep down, I knew.

It was me.

I was the soil.

Hard. Rocky. Distracted. Unready.

God kept planting His Word, His truth, His love... but I wasn't letting it sink in.

Then one day... I softened.

I let the plow break through the hard places.

I cleared the rocks and weeds.

I opened myself to the seed.

And slowly... life grew.

Roots stretched deep.

Green shoots appeared.

And eventually... a harvest.

Jesus told this story to remind us that our hearts matter.

The condition of our soil—the way we listen, trust, and follow—determines what grows.

I used to be stubborn soil.

But God never stopped planting.

And when I finally let Him in... everything changed.

## Reflection Questions:

1. What areas of your heart feel hard, distracted, or unready to receive God's Word?
2. How can you "prepare your soil" so your faith can grow?
3. What small steps can you take to stay open to God, even when it's hard?

## Prayer:

Dear God,
Sometimes my heart feels hard or distracted. But You never give up on me. Break through the stubborn places. Plant Your truth deep in my heart. Help my faith to grow strong—and bear fruit that lasts.
Amen.

## Key Verse (KJV):

"But he that received seed into the good ground is he that heareth the word, and understandeth it... and bringeth forth fruit."
— *Matthew 13:23*

# 34. I Let God's Word Take Root — And It Grew

*(Based on Matthew 13:3–9, 18–23, KJV — from the perspective of the good soil in the parable of the sower)*

---

I wasn't always good soil.

There were seasons when my heart was hard—nothing sank in.

Times when I was full of rocks—doubts, distractions, fear.

Moments when weeds of worry and comparison choked out everything God tried to plant.

But I wanted to change.

So, I let the Gardener work.

He broke up the hard places.

Pulled the weeds.

Cleared the stones.

Softened my soil.

Then, the seed came—the Word of God.

And this time… it stayed.

It sank deep.

It took root.

And slowly… it grew.

Faith doesn't sprout overnight. It's a process.

But as I listened to God's voice, obeyed His Word, and trusted His timing… fruit appeared.

Not just for me. For others too.

Jesus said when God's Word takes root in good soil, it produces a harvest—thirty, sixty, even a hundred times what was planted. I've seen that happen.
And I know... it's only the beginning.

## Reflection Questions:

1. How can you prepare your heart to be "good soil" for God's Word?
2. What small signs of spiritual growth have you seen in your life?
3. How can you stay rooted in God's truth, even when growth feels slow?

## Prayer:

Dear God,
Thank You for planting Your Word in my life. Help me to be good soil—to stay open, teachable, and ready to grow. Even when I don't see fruit right away, remind me that You're at work. Keep me rooted in You.
Amen.

## Key Verse (KJV):

"But he that received seed into the good ground is he that heareth the word, and understandeth it... and bringeth forth fruit."
— *Matthew 13:23*

## 35. I Ignored the Warning — And Faced the Flood

*(Based on Matthew 7:24–27, KJV — from the perspective of the foolish builder in the parable of the wise and foolish builders)*

---

The spot looked perfect.

Soft sand beneath my feet. Close to the water. Easy to build on.

Sure, the wise builder warned me.

"Storms will come," he said. "Build on the rock."

But the rock? That looked hard. Time-consuming. Uncomfortable.

The sand? It felt quick, convenient... good enough.

So, I ignored the warning.

I built my house fast. It looked great from the outside. For a while, I convinced myself I made the better choice.

Then the flood came.

The skies opened. The wind howled. The waves crashed.

And my house?

It collapsed.

Everything I built—gone in an instant.

Jesus told this story to remind us: ignoring His words feels easy... until the storms hit.

When life gets hard—when doubts, struggles, or pain come—what you've built your life on matters.

I learned the hard way.

Next time... I'll build on the Rock.

## Reflection Questions:

1. Are there areas of your life where you've been ignoring God's warnings or guidance?
2. What would it look like to build your life on God's truth instead of convenience?
3. How can you make small choices today to stand strong when storms come?

## Prayer:

Dear God,
It's tempting to take shortcuts or ignore Your voice. But I've seen how fragile life feels without You as my foundation. Help me not to build on sand. Teach me to follow Your Word, so I can stand strong no matter what comes.
Amen.

## Key Verse (KJV):

"And every one that heareth these sayings of mine, and doeth them not, shall be likened unto a foolish man, which built his house upon the sand."
— *Matthew 7:26*

## 36. I Was a Servant Waiting — And the Master Returned

*(Based on Luke 12:35–40, KJV — from the perspective of one of the faithful servants waiting for the master's return)*

༄

I didn't know when he'd come back.

The master had been gone for a long time. Days... weeks... it was easy to get distracted.

Some of the other servants stopped caring. They got lazy. They figured, "If the master isn't here, why bother?"

But I couldn't do that.

I stayed ready.

I kept the house in order.

I watched for his return.

I lit my lamp every night, just in case.

People laughed. "Why waste your time?" they said.

But deep down, I knew... he promised to return. And when he did, I wanted to be ready.

Then... it happened.

Late one night, the knock came. I opened the door—and there he stood.

The master smiled. "Well done," he said.

Jesus told this story to remind us that life isn't about killing time. It's about living ready.

I don't know the day or the hour.

But I know this...

I'll keep my lamp burning.

## Reflection Questions:

1. Have you ever felt tempted to stop caring or "drift" because God feels distant?
2. What does it look like to live ready for Jesus in your daily life?
3. How can you stay faithful, even when the waiting feels long?

## Prayer:

Dear God,
It's hard to wait sometimes. But I want to be faithful—to live ready for Your return. Help me to keep my lamp burning, my heart focused, and my life honoring You. Even when it feels slow, remind me that You always keep Your promises.
Amen.

## Key Verse (KJV):

"Blessed are those servants, whom the lord when he cometh shall find watching."
— *Luke 12:37a*

## 37. I Fell Asleep on Watch — And Missed My Moment

*(Based on Matthew 25:1–13, KJV — from the perspective of one of the bridesmaids who wasn't ready)*

~·~

At first, I was ready.

I had my lamp, my spot with the others, my excitement for the wedding.

But the waiting dragged on... and on... and on.

The night felt endless. The darkness thick. My eyelids heavy.

Somewhere along the way... I gave in.

I fell asleep.

When the shout finally came—"The bridegroom is here!"—I jolted awake in panic.

My lamp was empty. My oil was gone.

I scrambled to borrow some, but it was too late.

The others were ready. They followed the bridegroom in. The doors closed behind them.

I stood outside, heart sinking, realizing I'd missed my moment.

Jesus told this story to remind us that faith isn't a one-time spark—it's staying ready, even when life feels long or ordinary.

I thought I had time.

But I drifted. I dozed. And I missed it.

Next time... I'll stay awake.

## Reflection Questions:

1. Have you ever let spiritual distractions or "sleepiness" keep you from being ready for God?
2. What small choices help you stay alert and connected to your faith?
3. How can you live today like you're ready for God's next move?

## Prayer:

Dear God,
It's so easy to drift, to get distracted, to fall asleep in my faith. But I don't want to miss what You're doing. Wake me up. Keep me ready. Help me live every day prepared for You—with my lamp filled and my heart focused.
Amen.

## Key Verse (KJV):

"Watch therefore, for ye know neither the day nor the hour wherein the Son of man cometh."
— *Matthew 25:13*

## 38. I Tried to Hide My Sin — But the Truth Came Out

*(Based on Luke 12:1–3, KJV — from the perspective of someone who tried to hide their wrong choices)*

---

I thought no one would find out.

It was just a small lie. A shortcut. A hidden choice no one could see.

On the outside, I looked good. I smiled. I played the part. I even convinced myself it didn't matter.

But deep down?

I knew.

The guilt. The fear. The constant weight of wondering... *What if they find out?*

Jesus once said,

"There is nothing covered, that shall not be revealed; neither hid, that shall not be known."

At first, that scared me.

I worked harder to hide it. To cover up my mistakes.

But the truth? It has a way of rising to the surface.

Eventually... it did.

And honestly? It hurt.

But on the other side of truth... came freedom.

Hiding sin feels safe, but it traps you.

Confessing feels hard, but it sets you free.

Jesus doesn't expose us to shame us.

He reveals the truth... to heal us.

I tried to hide.

But now? I'd rather be free.

## Reflection Questions:

1. Have you ever tried to hide a mistake or sin, only to feel weighed down by it?
2. How does this story challenge you to live with honesty and integrity?
3. What step can you take to bring hidden things into the light and find freedom?

## Prayer:

Dear God,
I've tried to hide my mistakes, but You see it all. Thank You for loving me enough to call me into the light. Help me to be honest—with You, with myself, and with others. I don't want to live in fear. I want to live free.
Amen.

## Key Verse (KJV):

"For there is nothing covered, that shall not be revealed; neither hid, that shall not be known."
— *Luke 12:2*

# 39. I Stayed Humble — And God Lifted Me Up

*(Based on Luke 14:7–11, KJV — from the perspective of a guest at the banquet who chose humility)*

I almost chose the best seat.

When I walked into the banquet, the good seats were obvious—right by the host, front and center, where everyone could see you.

Part of me wanted that. To be noticed. To be important.

But I remembered what the Master had said:

"When you are bidden... sit down in the lowest room. For whosoever exalteth himself shall be abased; and he that humbleth himself shall be exalted."

So, I chose a quiet spot near the back. No spotlight. No attention.

Some people looked at me strangely. Others rushed to the front.

But then... the host arrived.

To my surprise, he approached me.

"Friend," he said, "move up higher."

He led me to a seat of honor.

Meanwhile, others who had claimed the best spots? They were asked to move down.

Jesus told this story to remind us: pride pushes us down... but humility lifts us up.

The world tells you to fight for the spotlight.

But God sees the quiet ones.

And in His time? He lifts them up.

## Reflection Questions:

1. Have you ever been tempted to chase attention or recognition?
2. What does true humility look like in your life?
3. How can you trust God to lift you up instead of forcing your own way?

## Prayer:

Dear God,
It's tempting to want recognition and praise. But You remind me that real greatness comes from humility. Help me to be content with quiet places, to trust Your timing, and to believe that You see me—even when others don't.
Amen.

## Key Verse (KJV):

"For whosoever exalteth himself shall be abased; and he that humbleth himself shall be exalted."
— *Luke 14:11*

## 40. I Took the Best Seat — And Was Sent Away

*(Based on Luke 14:7–11, KJV — from the perspective of a guest who tried to exalt himself at the banquet)*

---

I thought I deserved the best.

The banquet hall was packed, the room buzzing with conversation. As I walked in, I scanned the seats—the best ones were right by the host.

Without thinking twice, I marched over and sat down.

Front row. Full view. Everyone would see me here.

But the pride in my chest didn't last long.

The host approached... but not with a smile.

"Friend," he said gently, "this seat isn't for you. Please, move down."

The words stung. The eyes of the room were on me now—but not with admiration. With pity. With judgment.

I slid to the back, my face burning with embarrassment.

Jesus told this story to remind us: pride leads to a fall. Humility makes room for honor.

I wanted attention. But I missed the point.

Next time? I'll choose humility.

Let God do the lifting.

## Reflection Questions:

1. Have you ever chased recognition or praise, only to feel let down or embarrassed?
2. How does this story challenge your view of success or importance?
3. What small ways can you practice humility and let God lift you up in His time?

## Prayer:

Dear God,
Sometimes I get caught up in trying to be noticed or important. But You remind me that true greatness comes from humility. Help me to stop chasing the spotlight and trust You to place me where I belong. Teach me to be content, knowing You see me.
Amen.

## Key Verse (KJV):

"When thou art bidden, go and sit down in the lowest room... that when he that bade thee cometh, he may say unto thee, Friend, go up higher."
— *Luke 14:10*

# 41. I Sat at the Lowest Place — And Was Invited Higher

*(Based on Luke 14:7–11, KJV — from the perspective of a guest who chose humility at the banquet)*

---

The moment I walked into the banquet, I noticed the best seats. Right by the host. Front and center. Everyone would see you there.

Part of me wanted it.

But I remembered what the host had said before:

"Take the lowest place… let the host invite you higher."

So that's what I did.

I found a quiet spot near the back. Away from the spotlight. No attention. No fanfare.

Some guests gave me curious looks—maybe they thought I wasn't important enough to sit closer.

I stayed quiet.

Then… the host approached.

To my surprise, he stopped in front of me.

"Friend," he smiled, "move up higher."

He led me to a better seat. Not because I demanded it. Not because I forced it.

But because I waited.

Jesus told this story to show that God notices humility. You don't have to fight for position or attention.

In His time? He lifts you up.

## Reflection Questions:

1. Have you ever chosen humility, even when others seemed to chase the spotlight?
2. How does this story encourage you to trust God with your place and your future?
3. What does it look like to practice quiet confidence and humility in your life?

## Prayer:

Dear God,
Thank You for reminding me that I don't have to prove myself or fight for attention. Help me to choose humility, to trust You with my future, and to wait patiently for the places You've prepared for me. Lift me up in Your perfect time.
Amen.

## Key Verse (KJV):

"Friend, go up higher: then shalt thou have worship in the presence of them that sit at meat with thee."
— *Luke 14:10b*

## 42. I Judged Others — And Realized I Was Worse

*(Based on Matthew 7:1–5, KJV — from the perspective of someone who judged others before looking at their own faults)*

❦

I was quick to point fingers.

It was easy to spot other people's flaws—their bad choices, their attitudes, their mistakes.

"Look at him," I'd say.

"She's such a hypocrite."

"I'd never do that."

But Jesus' words echoed in my mind:

"Why beholdest thou the mote that is in thy brother's eye, but considerest not the beam that is in thine own eye?"

At first, I brushed it off.

But the more I thought about it, the more I saw... I was blind to my own mess.

The pride.

The jealousy.

The bitterness I carried.

While I judged others for tiny splinters... I was walking around with a whole plank in my eye.

I finally saw it.

Jesus wasn't saying never to help others grow—but to deal with my own heart first.

Judgment pushes people away.

Humility? It brings healing.

I used to judge.

Now, I'm learning to look inward first.

## Reflection Questions:

1. Have you ever been quick to judge others without noticing your own flaws?
2. How can you shift from criticizing to showing grace and understanding?
3. What does it look like to examine your own heart before trying to correct someone else?

## Prayer:

Dear God,
It's easy to judge others and ignore my own flaws. But You call me to humility, not hypocrisy. Help me to look inward first—to deal with my heart, my pride, and my attitudes. Teach me to lead with love, not judgment.
Amen.

## Key Verse (KJV):

"Thou hypocrite, first cast out the beam out of thine own eye; and then shalt thou see clearly to cast out the mote out of thy brother's eye."
— *Matthew 7:5*

## 43. I Removed the Plank — And Saw Clearly

*(Based on Matthew 7:1–5, KJV — from the perspective of someone who chose to deal with their own faults before judging others)*

---

I used to think I had perfect vision.

It was easy to spot other people's issues—their selfishness, their gossip, their drama.

I thought I saw it all so clearly.

But then Jesus' words hit me:

"First cast out the beam out of thine own eye; and then shalt thou see clearly..."

A beam? In my eye?

I laughed at first. But the more I thought about it, the more I realized... it was true.

My pride.

My impatience.

My tendency to judge without understanding.

It clouded my vision.

I was so focused on other people's tiny faults... I couldn't see my own.

So, I asked God to help me.

It wasn't easy. Seeing my flaws stung. But little by little, the beam came out.

And suddenly... I saw clearly.

Not to criticize. But to care.

Not to shame. But to show grace.

Not to tear down. But to build up.

Jesus wasn't saying ignore sin—He was saying start with yourself.

When I did?

Everything changed.

## Reflection Questions:

1. What "plank" or flaw in your life might be clouding how you see others?
2. How does dealing with your own struggles first help you love others better?
3. What does it mean to correct others with humility instead of judgment?

## Prayer:

Dear God,
Thank You for showing me that real change starts with my own heart. It's easy to focus on other people's flaws, but You call me to look inward first. Help me to deal with my struggles, so I can love and help others with humility and grace.
Amen.

## Key Verse (KJV):

"First cast out the beam out of thine own eye; and then shalt thou see clearly to cast out the mote out of thy brother's eye."
— *Matthew 7:5*

## 44. I Tried to Serve Two Masters — And It Broke Me

*(Based on Matthew 6:24, KJV — from the perspective of someone trying to follow God and the world at the same time)*

❦

I thought I could do both.

A little bit of God.

A little bit of chasing success.

A little bit of church.

A little bit of fitting in.

I figured if I balanced it right, no one would notice—and I could have the best of both worlds.

But Jesus' words echoed in my mind:

"No man can serve two masters... Ye cannot serve God and mammon."

I ignored it. At first.

But the cracks started to show.

I felt pulled in opposite directions.

Torn between faith and approval.

Between purpose and popularity.

Between peace and pressure.

The harder I tried to juggle it all... the more exhausted I became.

Until finally, I admitted it.

You can't serve two masters.

One will always win.

I realized the world offers quick rewards—but God offers lasting peace.

I chose Him.

And for the first time... I stopped feeling torn.

## Reflection Questions:

1. Have you ever felt pulled between following God and fitting into the world?
2. What "masters" compete for your attention, energy, and loyalty?
3. How can you choose to fully follow God, even when it costs something?

## Prayer:

Dear God,
I've tried to live with one foot in the world and one foot in faith—but it's exhausting. Help me to choose You completely. Teach me to let go of the things pulling me away from You. I want to serve You with my whole heart.
Amen.

## Key Verse (KJV):

"No man can serve two masters... Ye cannot serve God and mammon."
— *Matthew 6:24*

# 45. I Chased Riches — And Missed the Kingdom

*(Based on Luke 12:15–21, KJV — from the perspective of the rich man who built bigger barns)*

I thought I had it all figured out.

The harvest was massive. My barns? Too small to hold it all. So, I made a plan.

Tear them down. Build bigger ones. Store everything. Secure my future.

I told myself, "You've got it made. Eat, drink, be merry."

For a moment, I believed it.

But that night... I heard the words I never expected:

"Thou fool, this night thy soul shall be required of thee."

I froze.

All the wealth. All the success. All the careful planning.

None of it mattered now.

Jesus told this story to remind us that life isn't measured by possessions. You can gain the world and still lose your soul.

I thought building bigger barns would bring peace.

But I missed what really lasts.

I missed the Kingdom.

And now? I know...

True riches aren't stored on earth.

They're stored in heaven.

## Reflection Questions:

1. Have you ever chased success, money, or stuff, thinking it would satisfy you?
2. What does it mean to store up treasures in heaven instead of focusing on temporary things?
3. How can you shift your focus from chasing riches to growing in your faith?

## Prayer:

Dear God,
It's easy to get caught up in chasing success and stuff that won't last. But You remind me that true treasure is found in You. Help me to invest in things that matter—love, faith, kindness—and to trust You with my future.
Amen.

## Key Verse (KJV):

"So is he that layeth up treasure for himself, and is not rich toward God."
— *Luke 12:21*

## 46. I Trusted God with Little — And He Entrusted Me with More

*(Based on Matthew 25:14–30, KJV — from the perspective of the servant who received two talents and multiplied them)*

---

When the master handed me those two talents, I felt nervous.

It wasn't much compared to the guy who got five. But it wasn't nothing either.

I could've buried them. Played it safe. But something inside me knew... the master trusted me.

So, I got to work.

It wasn't flashy or impressive. Just small, steady steps.

Investing. Working hard. Using what I had.

Over time, the two talents grew into four.

I wasn't sure what the master would say when he returned. But when I placed the four talents in his hands, his face lit up.

"Well done, thou good and faithful servant," he said. "Thou hast been faithful over a few things, I will make thee ruler over many things."

That moment changed me.

Jesus told this story to remind us: it's not about how much you start with—it's about being faithful with what you have.

Small things matter.

And when you're faithful with little... God entrusts you with more.

## Reflection Questions:

1. Have you ever felt like what you have to offer is too small to matter?
2. What does being faithful with "little things" look like in your life?
3. How can you trust that God notices your quiet, consistent efforts?

## Prayer:

Dear God,
Sometimes I feel like what I have to offer isn't enough. But You remind me that small things matter. Help me to be faithful with what You've given me. Teach me to trust that You see my efforts, and that You will grow them in Your time.
Amen.

## Key Verse (KJV):

"Well done, thou good and faithful servant... thou hast been faithful over a few things, I will make thee ruler over many things."
— *Matthew 25:23*

## 47. I Doubted His Return — But He Came Suddenly

*(Based on Matthew 24:42–44, KJV — from the perspective of a servant who stopped watching for the master's return)*

---

At first, I was careful.

The master said he'd return—but didn't say when. So I stayed ready. I did my work. I paid attention.

But as time passed... I got lazy.

Days turned into weeks. Weeks into months. No sign of him.

I started thinking... *Maybe he's not coming back at all.*

I let my guard down. I slacked off. I stopped watching.

Then... it happened.

Out of nowhere, he returned.

The house was a mess. My work unfinished. I wasn't ready—and I couldn't hide it.

The look on his face?

Disappointment.

Jesus told this story to remind us: His return is real. And unexpected.

The world may tell you to relax, drift, forget.

But faith says... stay ready.

I doubted. I drifted. I wasn't prepared.

Next time... I'll watch.

## Reflection Questions:

1. Have you ever drifted in your faith because it felt like nothing was happening?
2. What daily habits can help you stay ready for Jesus, even when life feels ordinary?
3. How does knowing Jesus will return change how you live today?

## Prayer:

Dear God,
It's easy to get distracted and lose focus. But You remind me to stay ready. Help me not to drift or doubt, but to live with expectation and purpose. Keep me watchful and faithful, knowing You'll return in Your perfect timing.
Amen.

## Key Verse (KJV):

"Therefore be ye also ready: for in such an hour as ye think not the Son of man cometh."
— *Matthew 24:44*

## 48. I Held Onto the Seed — And It Never Grew

*(Based on John 12:24, KJV — from the perspective of a seed that refused to be planted)*

---

I was safe.

Tucked away in a jar. Untouched. Protected. Nothing could harm me there.

But nothing could grow either.

I watched other seeds fall to the ground—buried, forgotten. It looked terrifying.

But over time... I saw them sprout. Break through the soil. Stretch toward the sun.

Meanwhile, I stayed the same.

Safe.

Hidden.

Unchanged.

Jesus once said,

"Except a corn of wheat fall into the ground and die, it abideth alone: but if it die, it bringeth forth much fruit."

It hit me.

I was holding onto my life so tightly... I wasn't really living.

Growth requires surrender.

So, I took the risk.

I let go.

I fell into the soil.

I trusted the process.

And slowly... I changed.

What felt like the end... was the beginning.

Sometimes, dying to yourself—letting go of fear, pride, or comfort—is what it takes to truly grow.

## Reflection Questions:

1. Are you holding onto comfort, fear, or control in a way that's keeping you from growing?
2. What would it look like to "let go" and trust God with your life?
3. How can you embrace the uncomfortable parts of growth, knowing they lead to fruit?

## Prayer:

Dear God,
I like feeling safe and in control. But You remind me that real growth takes trust. Help me to let go of what's holding me back. Teach me to surrender my plans, my fears, and my comfort, so You can grow something beautiful in me.
Amen.

## Key Verse (KJV):

"Except a corn of wheat fall into the ground and die, it abideth alone: but if it die, it bringeth forth much fruit."
— *John 12:24*

# 49. I Let Go — And the Harvest Was Abundant

*(Based on John 12:24, KJV — from the perspective of the seed that chose to surrender and grow)*

---

I was buried.

Covered by dirt. Hidden from the light. For a moment, it felt like the end.

But it wasn't.

It was the beginning.

At first, I fought it. I wanted to stay safe, untouched, unchanged.

But deep down, I knew... seeds weren't made to stay buried.

They were made to grow.

Jesus once said,

"Except a corn of wheat fall into the ground and die, it abideth alone: but if it die, it bringeth forth much fruit."

So, I surrendered.

I let go of my old shell.

I pushed through the soil.

I reached for the sun.

It wasn't easy. Growth never is. But over time, I changed.

Roots dug deep.

Stems stretched tall.

And soon... fruit appeared.

Abundant. Overflowing.

Letting go felt scary.

But the harvest? It was worth it.

Jesus reminds us that surrender leads to life.

I let go.

And God did more than I ever imagined.

## Reflection Questions:

1. Have you ever resisted change because you were afraid to let go of comfort or control?
2. What does it mean for you to surrender your life to God in practical ways?
3. How does this story encourage you to trust that growth follows surrender?

## Prayer:

Dear God,
Change is scary. Letting go feels hard. But You remind me that real life begins when I surrender. Help me to trust You with my fears, my future, and my heart. Grow something beautiful in me as I let go and follow You.
Amen.

## Key Verse (KJV):

"But if it die, it bringeth forth much fruit."
— *John 12:24b*

# 50. I Cried for Justice — And God Answered in Time

*(Based on Luke 18:1–8, KJV — from the perspective of the persistent widow who kept asking for justice)*

---

People told me to give up.

The judge didn't care. He wasn't fair. He wasn't kind. He certainly wasn't in a hurry to help someone like me.

But I couldn't stay silent.

I had been wronged. Forgotten. Overlooked. But I wasn't going to stop crying out for justice.

So I went to the judge.

Day after day.

Week after week.

Refusing to give up.

At first, he ignored me. Rolled his eyes. Shut the door.

But I kept asking.

Finally, he had enough.

"Because this widow troubleth me, I will avenge her," he said.

Justice.

Jesus told this story to remind us: if even an unjust judge gives in eventually... how much more will a loving, righteous God answer His people when they cry out?

Sometimes, answers feel delayed.

But they're never forgotten.

God hears. God sees. And in His perfect time... God answers.

## Reflection Questions:

1. Have you ever prayed for something or cried out for justice but felt unheard?
2. How does this story remind you to keep trusting God, even when answers take time?
3. What area of your life do you need to be persistent in bringing before God?

## Prayer:

Dear God,
It's hard to wait. It's hard to feel unheard. But You remind me that You always listen, even when the answers take time. Give me faith to keep praying, strength to keep trusting, and peace to know You're always working behind the scenes.
Amen.

## Key Verse (KJV):

"And shall not God avenge his own elect, which cry day and night unto him... I tell you that he will avenge them speedily."
— *Luke 18:7–8a*

# 51. I Knocked and Knocked — And the Judge Heard Me

*(Based on Luke 18:1–8, KJV — from the perspective of the persistent widow focusing on her determination)*

❦

They called me annoying.

The woman who wouldn't quit. The one who kept showing up, knocking, asking, pleading.

But I didn't care.

I had been wronged. I needed justice. And the judge? He was the only one with the power to fix it.

At first, he ignored me.

Then he rolled his eyes.

Then he told me to go away.

But I stayed.

I knocked again.

And again.

And again.

Until finally… he caved.

"Because this widow troubleth me, I will avenge her," he muttered.

It wasn't because he cared about me—it was because I wouldn't quit.

Jesus told this story to remind us: if persistence works on an uncaring judge… imagine how much more your loving Father hears you.

You don't have to be perfect.

You don't have to have fancy prayers.

You just have to keep knocking.

God's not ignoring you.

He's listening.

And He will answer… in His perfect time.

## Reflection Questions:

1. Have you ever felt like giving up on prayer when nothing seemed to happen?
2. What helps you stay persistent in your prayers, even when it's hard?
3. How does this parable encourage you to keep knocking at God's door?

## Prayer:

Dear God,
Sometimes I get tired of asking. I wonder if You're listening. But You remind me to keep knocking, to keep trusting, to never give up. Help me believe that You hear every word, every cry, and that You will answer at the right time.
Amen.

## Key Verse (KJV):

"Men ought always to pray, and not to faint."
— *Luke 18:1b*

# 52. I Asked for Mercy — And God Gave It Freely

*(Based on Luke 18:9–14, KJV — from the perspective of the tax collector in the parable of the Pharisee and the tax collector)*

---

I couldn't even lift my eyes.

The temple was full of people. Some stood tall, proud, confident.

Me? I stood at the back. Head down. Heart heavy.

The Pharisee near the front prayed loud enough for everyone to hear:

"God, I thank thee that I am not as other men are…"

His words stung.

I knew I didn't measure up. My job? Hated. My reputation? Ruined. My heart? A mess.

But I was done pretending.

So I whispered the only prayer I could manage:

"God be merciful to me a sinner."

No fancy words. No excuses. Just raw honesty.

And that's when I felt it.

Mercy.

Grace.

Forgiveness.

Jesus said I went home justified… right with God.

Not because I was perfect.

But because I was real.

Because I asked.

God isn't impressed by pride.

But He always responds to humility.

## Reflection Questions:

1. Have you ever compared yourself to others instead of being honest with God?
2. What keeps you from bringing your failures and flaws to God?
3. How does this story remind you that God responds to humble, honest prayers?

## Prayer:

Dear God,
I mess up. I fall short. But You remind me that Your mercy isn't earned—it's given. Help me to come to You with honesty, not pride. Teach me to ask for Your forgiveness and to trust that You always welcome me with grace.
Amen.

## Key Verse (KJV):

"God be merciful to me a sinner."
— *Luke 18:13b*

## 53. I Thought I Was Righteous — But My Pride Was Exposed

*(Based on Luke 18:9–14, KJV — from the perspective of the Pharisee in the parable of the Pharisee and the tax collector)*

---

I thought I had it all together.

I prayed.

I tithed.

I followed the rules.

In my eyes? I was righteous.

So when I walked into the temple and saw the tax collector standing at the back, head down, I shook my head.

"Thank God I'm not like him," I whispered.

I listed my good deeds, proud and polished, confident that God must be impressed.

But Jesus saw right through me.

He said the tax collector—the one I looked down on—went home justified.

Me? I went home with nothing but pride.

I realized... all my good works meant nothing if my heart was full of comparison and pride.

Jesus wasn't impressed with my checklist.

He wanted humility. Honesty. Dependence on Him.

I thought I was righteous.

But my pride exposed how far I still had to go.

## Reflection Questions:

1. Have you ever fallen into the trap of comparing yourself to others spiritually?
2. What does this story teach you about pride versus true righteousness?
3. How can you shift your focus from impressing God to simply being honest with Him?

## Prayer:

Dear God,
It's so easy to compare, to measure, to judge. But You remind me that real faith isn't about appearances—it's about the heart. Help me to lay down my pride and come to You with humility, knowing that Your grace is all I need.
Amen.

## Key Verse (KJV):

"For every one that exalteth himself shall be abased; and he that humbleth himself shall be exalted."
— *Luke 18:14b*

## 54. I Came Broken — And Walked Away Whole

*(Based on Luke 18:9–14, KJV — from the perspective of the tax collector focusing on his restoration)*

༒

I didn't belong there.

The temple was for the holy, the polished, the people who got it right.

Me? I was a tax collector. Hated. Broken. Messed up.

But something pulled me there anyway.

I couldn't lift my head. I couldn't fake it.

While others prayed loud, proud prayers, I stood at the back, fists clenched, heart heavy.

All I could whisper was,

"God be merciful to me a sinner."

That's it.

No excuses. No promises to be perfect. Just honesty.

And Jesus said… I went home justified.

Forgiven.

Accepted.

Restored.

I came broken.

But I walked away whole.

Not because I earned it.

But because God's mercy is bigger than my mistakes.

## Reflection Questions:

1. Have you ever felt too broken or unworthy to come to God?
2. How does this story remind you that God welcomes honesty, not perfection?
3. What step can you take today to bring your brokenness to God and receive His mercy?

## Prayer:

Dear God,
Sometimes I feel too broken, too messy, too far gone. But You remind me that You don't turn me away. Thank You for welcoming me when I'm honest and real. Help me to come to You just as I am—and trust that Your mercy can make me whole. Amen.

## Key Verse (KJV):

"God be merciful to me a sinner."
— *Luke 18:13b*

## 55. I Wasted My Inheritance — But Found My Father's Arms Open

*(Based on Luke 15:11–24, KJV — from the perspective of the prodigal son)*

―✦―

I thought I had it all figured out.

I asked for my inheritance early—before my father even passed—and he gave it to me.

Freedom. Money. A chance to live life my way.

I left home and chased everything the world promised—parties, friends, fun.

But it didn't last.

The money ran out.

The friends disappeared.

I ended up feeding pigs... hungry enough to eat their slop.

That's when it hit me.

I had traded love for lies.

A home for heartbreak.

A future for failure.

But maybe... just maybe... I could go back.

I rehearsed my apology, ready to beg for a servant's job.

But before I even reached the door... my father ran to me.

He hugged me. He forgave me. He called me his son.

Jesus told this story to remind us: no matter how far you've run, God's arms are always open.

I wasted everything.

But His love? It never ran out.

## Reflection Questions:

1. Have you ever made choices that left you feeling lost or far from God?
2. What does this story show you about God's love, even when you mess up?
3. How can you take a step toward God today, knowing He welcomes you home?

## Prayer:

Dear God,
I've made mistakes. I've tried to do life my own way—and I've seen how empty it leaves me. But You remind me that Your arms are always open. Thank You for forgiving me and calling me Yours. Help me never to forget how much You love me. Amen.

## Key Verse (KJV):

"For this my son was dead, and is alive again; he was lost, and is found."
— *Luke 15:24a*

# 56. I Was the Older Brother — And Missed the Celebration

*(Based on Luke 15:25–32, KJV — from the perspective of the older brother in the parable of the prodigal son)*

---

I did everything right.

I stayed home. I worked hard. I followed the rules.

While my younger brother ran off and wasted everything, I stayed faithful. I kept the farm running. I honored our father.

But when my brother came crawling back... the celebration began.

A feast.

New clothes.

A ring on his finger.

And me? I stood outside. Angry. Bitter. Hurt.

"Why him?" I demanded. "I've been here all along."

But my father looked at me with love in his eyes.

"Son," he said, "you are always with me. All that I have is yours. But it's right to celebrate—your brother was lost, and now he's found."

In that moment, I realized... I was so focused on earning love, I forgot I already had it.

Jesus told this story to remind us: God's love isn't a competition.

It's a celebration—for the lost, for the found... for all of us.

## Reflection Questions:

1. Have you ever struggled with jealousy or bitterness when others receive grace?
2. How does this story remind you that God's love isn't about earning—it's about relationship?
3. What step can you take to join in celebrating others, even when it's hard?

## Prayer:

Dear God,
Sometimes I compare. I try to earn love. I get jealous when others receive grace. But You remind me that Your love is for all of us. Help me to let go of pride, to join the celebration, and to remember that I've always had a place with You.
Amen.

## Key Verse (KJV):

"For this thy brother was dead, and is alive again; and was lost, and is found."
— *Luke 15:32*

# 57. I Looked for the Lost — And Discovered God's Heart

*(Based on Luke 15:3–7, KJV — from the perspective of the shepherd searching for the lost sheep)*

❦

I could've stayed with the ninety-nine.

They were safe. Accounted for. It would've been easier to settle for almost everyone being okay.

But I couldn't.

One was missing.

One sheep lost in the wilderness. Wandering. Alone.

It might sound foolish to leave ninety-nine for one. But to me? Every sheep matters.

So, I searched.

Through hills and valleys. Over rocks and underbrush. Calling. Listening.

Finally... I found him.

Shivering. Scared. Stuck.

I didn't scold him. I lifted him onto my shoulders and carried him home.

And when I arrived? I celebrated.

Jesus told this story to remind us: God's heart is for the lost. The one who wandered. The one overlooked. The one others might forget.

I looked for the lost.

And in doing so… I understood God's love a little more.

Because that's what He does for me.

## Reflection Questions:

1. Have you ever felt lost, overlooked, or forgotten like the sheep in this story?
2. How does this parable remind you of God's relentless love and pursuit?
3. What small ways can you reflect God's heart by looking out for someone who feels lost?

## Prayer:

Dear God,
Thank You for searching for me when I've wandered. Your love never gives up. Help me to see others through Your eyes—to notice the lost, to care for them, and to remind them they matter to You.
Amen.

## Key Verse (KJV):

"Rejoice with me; for I have found my sheep which was lost."
— *Luke 15:6b*

## 58. I Believed God's Kingdom Was Near — And I Prepared My Heart

*(Based on Matthew 25:1–13, KJV — from the perspective of one of the wise bridesmaids who was ready for the bridegroom)*

❦

I didn't know when he would arrive.

No one did.

But I believed the bridegroom was coming.

So, I prepared.

I made sure my lamp had oil. I checked it again and again. Some of the others laughed, told me to relax, said I was overthinking it.

But I couldn't take the chance.

The hours dragged on. The sky grew dark. We all got drowsy.

But when the cry rang out—

"The bridegroom is coming!"

—I was ready.

I grabbed my lamp, lit the flame, and stepped into the night.

Some of the others scrambled for oil… but it was too late.

Jesus told this story to remind us: His kingdom is near. We may not know the hour, but we can live prepared.

I believed.

I prepared.

And when He came… I was ready.

## Reflection Questions:

1. How can you prepare your heart daily to be ready for God's plans?
2. What distractions or doubts sometimes keep you from living ready?
3. How does this parable remind you that faith is both believing and preparing?

## Prayer:

Dear God,
Sometimes I forget how near You are. But You remind me to be ready—not in fear, but in faith. Help me to live prepared, to keep my lamp burning, and to stay focused on You. I want to be ready when You call.
Amen.

## Key Verse (KJV):

"Watch therefore, for ye know neither the day nor the hour wherein the Son of man cometh."
— *Matthew 25:13*

## 59. I Planted Seeds — And Watched God Bring the Growth

*(Based on Mark 4:26–29, KJV — from the perspective of the farmer in the parable of the growing seed)*

⁓✻⁓

I've planted seeds before.

But it still amazes me every time.

I scatter them across the soil. I water them. I wait.

But what happens next? That part isn't up to me.

Day and night, while I sleep... they grow.

First, tiny sprouts break through the soil. Then stems. Then leaves. And eventually... the harvest.

I can't explain how it happens. But it does.

Jesus told this story to remind us: God's kingdom grows the same way.

You plant kindness.

You share your faith.

You live with love.

You may not see results right away.

But quietly... steadily... God works beneath the surface.

Before long, hearts change.

Lives grow.

The harvest comes.

It's not about forcing it.

It's about planting seeds... and trusting God with the growth.

## Reflection Questions:

1. Have you ever felt discouraged when you didn't see immediate results from doing good?
2. What "seeds" of faith, love, or kindness can you plant today?
3. How can you trust that even when you don't see it, God is working behind the scenes?

## Prayer:

Dear God,
Sometimes I want to see results right away. But You remind me that growth takes time. Help me to keep planting good seeds—through my words, my actions, and my faith—and trust You to bring the harvest in Your perfect timing.
Amen.

## Key Verse (KJV):

"And should sleep, and rise night and day, and the seed should spring and grow up, he knoweth not how."
— *Mark 4:27*

## 60. I Was the Fig Tree — And God Gave Me Another Chance

*(Based on Luke 13:6–9, KJV — from the perspective of the fig tree in the parable)*

---

I was supposed to produce fruit.

That's why I was planted. That's why I stood in the garden—rooted, growing, reaching for the sun.

But year after year... nothing.

The owner came, looking for figs.

He found leaves.

Branches.

But no fruit.

I saw the frustration in his eyes.

"Cut it down," he said. "Why should it take up space?"

My heart sank. I had wasted the soil. Wasted the chance. I didn't deserve to stay.

But the gardener... he spoke up.

"Give it one more year," he pleaded. "I'll dig around it. Fertilize it. Care for it. If it bears fruit, good. If not... then cut it down."

I couldn't believe it.

Another chance.

Jesus told this story to remind us: God is patient—but He longs for growth in our lives.

We weren't made to just take up space.

We were made to grow.

To bear fruit.

To reflect His love.

I almost gave up.

But God didn't.

And now... I'm ready to grow.

## Reflection Questions:

1. Are there areas of your life where you've been stuck or unfruitful?
2. How does this story remind you of God's patience and desire for growth?
3. What small step can you take today to bear fruit in your faith?

## Prayer:

Dear God,
Thank You for being patient with me when I fall short. You could've given up—but You didn't. Help me to grow, to change, and to bear fruit for You. Teach me to use this second chance well.
Amen.

## Key Verse (KJV):

"Lord, let it alone this year also, till I shall dig about it, and dung it."
— *Luke 13:8*

# Closing Note from the Author

Dear Reader,

Thank you for walking through these stories with me.

Maybe you've heard some of these parables before—or maybe they felt brand new. Either way, I hope they reminded you of something simple but easy to forget:

God's truth isn't hidden in complicated places.
It's tucked into the ordinary.
In fields. At tables. In lost things and found things.
And most importantly—in you.

Jesus used stories not to confuse us, but to invite us closer. To help us see that no matter who we are or what we've been through, hope is never out of reach. Growth is always possible. And faith? It often starts with small steps—listening, wondering, believing.

So if life feels uncertain, or your faith feels messy, remember this:
The same God who told these stories is still writing yours.

And in His hands, even the smallest seed can grow into something incredible.

Keep listening.
Keep growing.
And never forget—you are part of God's story, too.

With hope,
**G. Jordan**

# Acknowledgments

Every book is a team effort—even the quiet ones written in the early mornings or late at night.

First, I thank God—the ultimate storyteller—who weaves grace, hope, and redemption into lives far beyond what we deserve. The parables of Jesus have shaped my heart for years, and it's a privilege to help retell them for a new generation.

To the teens who ask honest questions, wrestle with their faith, and keep showing up anyway—you inspired these pages more than you know. Your curiosity, doubts, and courage to grow remind me daily why stories still matter.

To my family and friends—thank you for cheering me on, praying for me, and reminding me that simple faith is often the strongest faith.

To every teacher, youth leader, and mentor who believes in young hearts and plants seeds of truth—you may never see the full harvest, but God does. This book is part of that harvest.

And finally, to the quiet readers—the ones who picked up this book looking for answers or hope—I see you. More importantly, God sees you. Keep listening. Keep leaning in. Your story matters.

Thank you all.

— G. Jordan

# About the Author

G. Jordan is a faith-based author committed to helping young readers engage with Scripture in a meaningful and accessible way. Through the 10-Minute Bible Stories for Teens series, G. Jordan combines biblical accuracy with relatable storytelling, offering teens practical insights for navigating life, faith, and relationships.

Having spent years living in Malaysia, Singapore, the United States, and Australia, G. Jordan brings a global perspective to their writing. This international background has shaped a deep appreciation for the diverse ways teens experience faith, community, and friendship across cultures.

With a focus on short, reflective devotionals, G. Jordan's work encourages teenagers to explore the challenges and triumphs of well-known and lesser-known Bible characters. Each book in the series is designed to foster spiritual growth, personal reflection, and a deeper understanding of God's love and purpose.

G. Jordan's writing is grounded in a desire to make the timeless truths of the Bible approachable for today's generation.

# Books in This Series

| | |
|---|---|
|  | 10-Minute Bible Stories for Teens: Voices of Courage, Doubt, and Grace<br>ASIN: B0F9VKYFTW<br>ISBN: 9798285150350 |
|  | 10-Minute Bible Friendships for Teens: Stories of Loyalty, Forgiveness, and Love<br>ASIN: B0FFTRLGV8<br>ISBN: 9798289539878 |
|  | 10-Minute Bible Parables for Teens: Stories of Hope, Growth, and Faith<br>ASIN: B0FGX6YV8K<br>ISBN: 9798291237083 |

## We'd Love to Hear from You!

Thank you for spending time with *10-Minute Bible Parables for Teens: Stories of Hope, Growth, and Faith.* We hope these short, relatable stories have encouraged your heart, strengthened your faith, and reminded you that God's truth is always relevant — even in life's small, everyday moments.

If this book has blessed you or helped you grow, would you consider leaving a short review on Amazon?

### Your review makes a difference.

- It helps other teens and families discover this book.
- It encourages us to keep creating resources that inspire faith and hope.
- It lets us know what you found meaningful — and what you'd love to see more of.

Leaving a review takes just a minute, but it means the world to us.

### Simply visit Amazon and share your honest thoughts.
It doesn't have to be long — even one or two sentences is a huge help!

*"Your feedback not only supports this book — it helps share God's message with others."*

Thank you so much for being part of this journey.
Keep growing. Keep believing. Keep shining.

Printed in Dunstable, United Kingdom